Government-Sponsored Enterprises

Government-Sponsored Enterprises

Mercantilist Companies in the Modern World

Thomas H. Stanton

The AEI Press

Publisher for the American Enterprise Institute
WASHINGTON, D.C.

2002

Available in the United States from the AEI Press, c/o Publisher Resources Inc., 1224 Heil Quaker Blvd., P.O. Box 7001, La Vergne, TN 37086-7001. To order, call 1-800-269-6267. Distributed outside the United States by arrangement with Eurospan, 3 Henrietta Street, London WC2E 8LU, England.

Library of Congress Cataloging-in-Publication Data

Stanton, Thomas H., 1944–
    Government-sponsored enterprises : mercantilist companies in the modern world /
    Thomas H. Stanton.
        p. cm.
    Includes bibliographical references and index.
    ISBN 0-8447-4160-4 (cloth)
        1. Government-sponsored enterprises—United States. 2. Public-private sector cooperation—United States. 3. Loans—United States—Government guaranty. 4. Subsidies—United States. I. Title

HG181 .S7928 2001
338.7′4′0973—dc21

                                                                        2001053626

1 3 5 7 9 10 8 6 4 2

THE AEI PRESS
Publisher for the American Enterprise Institute
1150 17th Street, N.W., Washington, D.C. 20036

Printed in the United States of America

To Marty, Benjamin, and Joshua

Contents

Foreword

A fundamental revolution has been under way in the operation of the public sector since World War II both in the United States and increasingly in other parts of the world. The heart of the revolution is a transformation not just in the scope and scale of government action but also in its basic *forms*—in the *tools* of public action, the *instruments* or means used to address public problems. Where government activity was once restricted primarily to the direct delivery of goods or services, it now embraces a dizzying array of loans, loan guarantees, grants, contracts, social regulation, economic regulation, insurance, tax expenditures, and vouchers.

What is more, many of the most rapidly expanding tools share a common feature: they are highly *indirect*. They rely on a wide assortment of third parties—commercial banks, private hospitals, social service agencies, industrial corporations, universities, day-care centers, other levels of government, financiers, construction firms—to deliver publicly financed services and pursue publicly authorized purposes. The upshot is an elaborate system of *third-party government* in which crucial elements of public authority are shared with a host of nongovernmental or other-governmental actors, frequently in complex collaborative systems that sometimes defy comprehension, let alone effective management and control. In a sense the public administration problem has leapt beyond the borders of the public agency and now embraces a wide assortment of third parties intimately engaged in the implementation of the public's business.

What is involved here, moreover, is not simply the delegation of clearly defined ministerial duties to closely regulated agents of the state. What is distinctive about many of the newer tools of public action is that they share with third-party actors a far more basic governmental function: the exercise of discretion over the use of public authority and the spending of public funds. Under many of them a major share—in many cases *the* major share—of the discretion over the operation of public programs routinely comes to rest not with the governmental agencies authorizing the action but with the third-party actors that actually carry them out.

Among the new tools of public action, none is more curious, more obscure, and more difficult to penetrate than the government-sponsored enterprise. Not quite a private-sector company, yet not quite a government agency, the GSE occupies a strange netherworld of organizational life rarely visited by any but the most intrepid explorers.

Fortunately for us, Tom Stanton is one of those explorers, and he has given us a rare look into the unexamined continent. What he reports is truly extraordinary. From often meager roots as experimental instrumentalities designed to correct some market imperfection—usually in the capital markets—GSEs have parlayed their quasi-public status into huge enterprises that now own or underwrite nearly half of all single-family conventional mortgages, more than a quarter of all farm credit, and more than a quarter of all student loans. What is more, Stanton makes clear that GSEs are not all that new: their structure and their role mirror those of the mercantilist enterprises of sixteenth- and seventeenth-century Europe. Unlike the government-backed merchant monopolies of that earlier era, however, America's GSEs have refused to fade away. To the contrary, they have skillfully used their implicit access to publicly backed credit to compete effectively in the commercial marketplace and often reap sizable profits for their private investors.

Whether today's government-sponsored enterprises deserve to retain their government backing is a matter of intense dispute. Stanton concludes that in today's efficient capital markets the need for such a set of institutions has generally disappeared. However one feels about the issue, this study reminds us of the often strange and inventive forms that public action takes and cautions us about the dangers to democratic control that such inventiveness, for all its virtues, can sometimes entail, particularly when it takes an institutional form.

Lester M. Salamon
Director
Center for Civil Society Studies
Johns Hopkins University

Preface

The U.S. government has created many different kinds of institutions to carry out public purposes. Of these, government-sponsored enterprises are among the most interesting. The six GSEs are financial institutions: Fannie Mae, Freddie Mac, and the Federal Home Loan Bank System in housing, the Farm Credit System and Farmer Mac in agriculture, and Sallie Mae in student loans. Their financial, structural, and legal attributes provide many lessons for policymakers and policy analysts. The analysis of GSEs can shed light on issues of institutional design and the need for policymakers to pay increased attention to the structure and quality of the organizations that they attempt to create through the legislative process.

Harold Seidman has pointed out that the choice of institutional form can have substantial implications for the way that public purposes are carried out.[1] As instruments of government policy, GSEs provide instructive case studies of the consequences of design choices for the strengths and limitations and life cycles of a particular type of institution.[2]

GSEs are hybrids that combine the characteristics of public and private organizations. Their ownership and their control are private, but the government provides them significant subsidies, including tax and regulatory advantages, and permits them to fund their activities almost as if they were part of the government. The GSEs operate in markets where their non-GSE competitors do not receive such benefits.

For policy analysts who believe that history helps to explain current institutional behavior, the study of GSEs can offer special insights. The lineal ancestors of today's GSEs—including the first and second Banks of the United States and even earlier institutions from mercantilist times—also manifested the peculiar mixture of public purpose and private profitability that motivates GSEs in today's world. Because of the size and long life cycles of some GSEs, patterns of their behavior can also illuminate issues of governance. This book explores the contrast in behavior and evolution between investor-owned GSEs and GSEs that are structured to be cooperatives.

Finally, students of the law, including myself, may become fascinated with the unusual legal framework of GSEs. It is the thesis of this study that much as the law shapes institutions of government, so too does the peculiar legal framework of GSEs determine much of their behavior. GSEs are an excellent case study of the development of the law and the age-old question of the relationship between economic factors and legal factors in the development of legal and economic systems. GSEs are an old institutional form that has taken on new vitality because of political strength that protects their government subsidies and allows them to expand in the marketplace.

Thus the study of GSEs offers multiple insights. Some lessons that I have derived from my study of GSEs over the years include the following:

- *Development of law.* Except in unusual times, such as the decade of the Great Depression and the New Deal in the United States, the law tends to lag developments in the marketplace; elements of legal design that were beneficial in one set of economic circumstances may become irrelevant or even harmful later.
- *Financial risk.* The relative flexibility of the private sector vis-à-vis the public sector, again except for unusual times, permits private companies to engineer their financial activities to deal with almost any requirement of government regulations. The situation gives rise to an iron law of legislative design for financial regulators, programs, and institutions: financial risk migrates to the place where the government is least equipped to deal with it.[3]
- *Mixture of public and private attributes in a single institution.* Lawmakers cannot predict the myriad of economic circumstances that may emerge in fast-moving markets. That predicament makes it difficult to design an organization that combines public and private attributes and to ensure that the organization can serve public purposes over its lifetime. By contrast it is potentially much easier to design a simple and effective direct subsidy for a government program or a private activity.[4]

- *Life cycle.* Designing an institution to carry out public purposes requires close attention to the likely life cycle of the institution and must include a workable exit strategy.

In short, this book is about the institutional design and the structure of the GSE as a special type of institution authorized, defined, and shaped by law. The individual GSEs provide examples to inform the analysis. Readers who want access to literature relating to other institutions that carry out public purposes might visit the website of the Standing Panel on Executive Organization and Management of the National Academy of Public Administration.[5] That site focuses on governmental institutions that help to provide a counterpoint to the private institutions, such as GSEs, that the government charters to carry out public purposes.

I would like to express gratitude to reviewers of parts or all of an earlier draft of this book. Daniel Guttman, Ronald Moe, Gary Norton, David Roderer, Harold Seidman, Robert S. Seiler Jr., William B. Shear, and Peter J. Wallison contributed numerous insights. I am grateful for their detailed feedback and sometimes extensive comments. Although I have benefited from many of the reviewers' suggestions, I remain solely responsible for the contents of this volume.

The design of public institutions can be understood in terms of perhaps six discrete sets of issues:

- the organizational form of the institution (involving issues as to whether the organization is public, private, or hybrid);
- the nature of the subsidies that the government provides to the institution as its tool;[6]
- the public purposes of the institution;
- the history of similar institutions;
- the institution's governance structure and life cycle; and
- the exit strategy for the institution when it has served or otherwise outlived its usefulness as an instrument of public policy.

The seven chapters of this book include a general overview of GSEs and one chapter focusing on each set of design issues. The first chapter provides an overview of the size and activities of the GSEs today, their institutional behavior, and origins. The second chapter begins the analysis of legal attributes and organizational form of the GSE and the important differences between GSEs and other private companies. That chapter introduces the legal concept of the instrumentality of government, a nongovernmental organization that serves public purposes.

GSEs are a special type of instrumentality: chapter 3 examines the most distinctive feature of GSE status, the implicit government backing for GSE obligations. The government seems to encounter difficulties in administering that unusual subsidy compared with other, more direct types of subsidy.

Thanks to the perceived government backing, GSEs operate with higher financial leverage and less capital than other firms in similar lines of business and thus with a significant competitive advantage in the marketplace. A private company such as a commercial bank or an insurance company may not be able to compete against the special subsidies and preferences that the government provides for a GSE. But the perception of government backing means that the government should supervise the safety and soundness of the GSEs.

Chapter 4 looks at the public purposes of the individual GSEs as reflected in their enabling legislation. The chapter reviews the charter powers of the major GSEs and how those powers have expanded, assesses the government oversight of the GSEs' public purposes, and discusses the impact of new technologies on GSEs' activities authorized by their charters.

The fifth chapter traces the peculiar legal framework of GSEs to the origins in the first Bank of the United States and, before that, the Bank of England. The legal structure of the GSE is a vestige of mercantilist Europe, when a sovereign would grant a special charter to a company to undertake special activities. The behavior of GSEs today, especially because of their incentives to protect their favorable legal status by dominating the political process, resembles the behavior of earlier mercantilist institutions.

Chapter 6 offers a case study of the consequences of institutional design for the life cycles of GSEs. It begins with an analysis of the tension between private profits and public purposes that GSEs were designed to serve. Then the chapter contrasts two investor-owned GSEs, Fannie Mae and Freddie Mac, with the third housing GSE, the cooperatively owned Federal Home Loan Bank System. While an investor-owned GSE attempts to increase profitability by expanding into new markets, a cooperative such as the Federal Home Loan Bank System can be limited by the power of its members and the need to serve their interests. Finally, the seventh chapter discusses issues relating to the design of an exit strategy for GSEs, including lessons that can be derived from 1996 legislation to restructure Sallie Mae, remove its federal sponsorship, and end its GSE status.

Based on my study of GSEs over many years, I conclude that GSEs once provided valuable benefits but that the special-purpose GSE charter does not suit today's fast-moving financial markets, particularly in the United States and other developed economies. Markets are changing so quickly that the GSE becomes a long-term institutional solution for a problem that may be quite transitory. To the extent that the GSEs have improved markets through their innovations and development of economies of scale, they have diminished the need for the government to continue to develop such markets through special forms of intervention and subsidy such as a GSE.

The government-sponsored enterprise is an important instrument of government policy. As Lester Salamon has pointed out in his seminal work on tools of government, "the key is to fit the tool to the nature of the task."[7] Absent serious institutional shortcomings in both the government and the private markets, a GSE seems a poor fit in today's marketplace. To the extent that a GSE is chartered to serve purposes defined by law, it can lack the flexibility of a completely private financial services firm that is free to define and redefine its activities and lines of business in response to market signals. To the extent that a GSE wields market power, it can impede the emergence of more efficient competitors and innovations. To the extent that a GSE uses its access to government subsidies to expand its market power, it imposes burdens on market competition that would not be present if the government provided comparable subsidies without tying these benefits and preferences to a handful of institutions.

The poor fit is made worse to the extent that government has abdicated to the GSEs themselves the power to affect the public benefits and public costs of GSEs. In the early stages of Fannie Mae and Freddie Mac, the government kept fairly tight control over the organizations. Until 1989 Fannie Mae was limited by its charter to providing "supplementary assistance" to the secondary mortgage market. The Department of Housing and Urban Development, Fannie Mae's designated government supervisor, had the authority to approve any new activity. Freddie Mac was governed by a board of three government officials who also served as members of the Federal Home Loan Bank Board.

Over time the law has changed and has reduced government control. Today Fannie Mae's charter authority has expanded to permit it to "respond appropriately to the private capital market," and HUD has given up its authority of prior approval over Fannie Mae's activities. Shareholders, rather than government officials, now control Freddie Mac's board of directors. The changes took place in the context of a legislative environment distracted by larger events such as the savings and loan debacle and financial difficulties with major HUD programs. The government seemed virtually unaware of the extent to which it was losing control over the largest GSEs. Chapter 4 offers numerous other examples of the expanded scope and extent of permitted GSE activities.

For those reasons and in contrast to my position some years ago,[8] I now believe that government must devise an exit strategy for the GSEs. Given the controversy about GSEs today, not all readers may agree with my policy conclusion. This book is intended to serve all readers regardless of their view on such ultimate questions by providing a guide to the legal and institutional framework that shapes GSEs and their behavior. The notes are intended to help readers of all persuasions carry out their own research into the fascinating and unusual institutions known as government-sponsored enterprises.

1

Mercantilist Institutions in the Marketplace

Government-sponsored enterprises are some of the largest and most profitable financial institutions in the United States. Fannie Mae and Freddie Mac fund more than $1 trillion of home mortgages each; together, the twelve Federal Home Loan Banks fund $654 billion of mortgages and nonmortgage investments; banks and associations of the Farm Credit System hold $94 billion of agricultural loans and other assets; and Sallie Mae holds $49 billion of student loans and other assets. The smallest of the GSEs, called Farmer Mac, is large compared with many other rural financial institutions; it funds about $4.7 billion of agricultural and rural loans and other investments. In concept the charters of the GSEs—except the Farm Credit System and Farmer Mac—limit the entities to serving the secondary market: they may not originate loans directly to borrowers but instead must purchase or otherwise fund the home mortgages, student loans, or other loans, as the case may be.

From the perspective of institutional design, the GSEs possess two characteristics that, taken together, distinguish them from all other institutional types. First, unlike ordinary private corporations, the GSEs operate under unique federal charters rather than under the business corporation laws of a state. They are designed to serve public purposes that are defined by laws that limit their activities. Second, the GSEs benefit from the perception that the government stands behind their financial obligations. The combination of the characteristics also contributes to the GSEs' growth.

The unusual statutory framework of GSEs gives rise to the following definition: a government-sponsored enterprise is a privately owned, federally chartered financial institution with nationwide

1

scope and specialized lending powers that benefits from an implicit federal guarantee of all its obligations to enhance its ability to borrow money.[1] The definition is consistent with, but slightly narrower than, the statutory definition in the Congressional Budget Act of 1974, as amended in 1990.[2] Under that definition federal law has established today's six GSEs:

- Farm Credit System (FCS)[3]
- Federal Home Loan Bank System (FHLBS)[4]
- Federal National Mortgage Association (Fannie Mae)[5]
- Federal Home Loan Mortgage Corporation (Freddie Mac)[6]
- Student Loan Marketing Association (Sallie Mae)[7]
- Federal Agricultural Mortgage Corporation (Farmer Mac)[8]

Federal law has established two institutions that resemble GSEs in their financial characteristics but are effectively owned and controlled by the government rather than private owners.[9] The government created the two, the Financing Corporation (FICO)[10] and the Resolution Funding Corporation (REFCORP),[11] to fund the bailout of the failed savings and loan industry with billions of dollars that would not appear in the federal budget. Under current budget rules rather than the rules that applied when the two institutions were created in the 1980s, their borrowings and outlays would now appear in the federal budget. This book does not discuss the two institutions except in passing.

As discussed in chapter 2, the GSE is a privately owned and privately controlled instrumentality of government. The government charters each GSE, gives it special benefits and subsidies, and attempts to direct its activities to serve high-priority public purposes in sectors, such as housing and agriculture, that policymakers believe are not adequately served by private capital. The GSE is to use its benefits and subsidies to further its government-authorized activities.

The major government benefit is the authority to borrow money in the so-called agency credit market at rates close to Treasury's. The benefit derives from a perception that the government stands behind the obligations of each GSE. That perception, discussed in chapter 3, permits each GSE to borrow huge amounts of money. Low capital standards compared with other financial institutions permit each GSE to maintain higher leverage—sometimes much higher leverage—than if there were no perception of government backing. The federal government attempts to oversee the GSEs' service to public purposes and also attempts to supervise the safety and soundness of each GSE. Chapters 2 and 3, respectively, discuss those issues.

Thanks to their special government benefits, GSEs have rapidly grown and now dominate many market segments, especially in housing (Fannie Mae, Freddie Mac, and the Federal Home Loan Banks) and student loans (Sallie Mae). A 1999 report by the Congressional Research Service speaks of Fannie Mae and Freddie Mac as a "subsidized monopoly (or duopoly)."[12] Although the Farm Credit System also is large, its size has been kept in check by the economic conditions in rural America and also by rural banks that can compete effectively against FCS institutions. Table 1-1 shows that most GSEs are huge institutions:

TABLE 1-1
GSEs BY SIZE AND FUNCTION

GSE	Year Authorized as a GSE	Public Purpose	Size at Year-End 2000
Farm Credit System	1916	Lend to agriculture	$94 billion (assets)
Federal Home Loan Bank System	1932	Lend to financial institutions to fund mortgages	$654 billion (assets)
Fannie Mae (Federal National Mortgage Association)	1968	Serve the secondary home mortgage market— fund mortgages	$607 billion (assets) plus $707 billion (mortgage-backed securities guaranteed)
Freddie Mac (Federal Home Loan Mortgage Corporation)	1970	Serve the secondary home mortgage market— fund mortgages	$386 billion (assets) plus $576 billion (mortgage-backed securities guaranteed)
Sallie Mae (Student Loan Marketing Association)	1972	Serve the secondary market for student loans— fund student loans	$48.8 billion (assets)
Farmer Mac (Federal Agricultural Mortgage Corporation)	1987	Fund agricultural mortgages	$3.2 billion (assets) plus $1.5 billion (mortgage-backed securities guaranteed)

SOURCE: GSE annual reports and information statements, 2000.

GSEs in the Marketplace

Each GSE began as a small institution; most of them remained small for a number of years before establishing themselves in the market. The largest GSEs—those serving the housing market—have grown at a pace that would make private firms envious. On average, Fannie Mae and Freddie Mac have *more than doubled in size every five years* since the government chartered Freddie Mac in 1970. Table 1-2 shows the growth of the two GSEs, including their outstanding debt obligations plus outstanding mortgage-backed securities, between 1970 and 2000. The Federal Home Loan Banks have also grown rapidly in terms of their consolidated obligations outstanding (table 1-3).

The growth of the Farm Credit System was rapid until the serious agricultural recession in the early 1980s. As table 1-4 shows (again in terms of obligations outstanding), the FCS has resumed its growth, but at a more moderate pace. Sallie Mae has doubled in size every five years (again in terms of GSE obligations outstanding). Its growth rate then diminished as the GSE sought and in 1996 received the authority to transform itself into a company that would ultimately operate without government sponsorship (see table 1-5).

The dramatic expansion of the GSEs has been a part of a pattern of large-scale federalization of certain sectors of the economy. Agriculture and student loans have long been federalized through pervasive agricultural income and credit programs and the federal

TABLE 1-2
GROWTH OF FANNIE MAE AND FREDDIE MAC, 1970–2000

Year	Obligations
1970	$15.2 billion
1975	$37.2 billion
1980	$76.6 billion
1985	$261.3 billion
1990	$768.0 billion
1995	$1.3 trillion
2000	$2.4 trillion

SOURCE: Congressional Budget Office, *Controlling the Risks of Government-Sponsored Enterprises* (Washington, D.C.: Government Printing Office, 1991), table 3, p. 12; and Office of Federal Housing Enterprise Oversight, *2001 Report to Congress* (Washington, D.C.: Government Printing Office, 2001), table 24, p. 78.

TABLE 1-3
GROWTH OF FHLB, 1970–2000

Year	Obligations
1970	$10.5 billion
1975	$16.4 billion
1980	$37.3 billion
1985	$75.6 billion
1990	$117.9 billion
1995	$231.4 billion
2000	$591.6 billion

SOURCE: CBO, *Controlling the Risks*, and FHLBS annual financial statements, 1970–2000.

student assistance programs, including both guaranteed and direct student loans. In 1982, at its peak in terms of market share, the Farm Credit System held 34 percent of total farm debt outstanding. At year-end 1999 the FCS had a market share of about 27 percent.[13] At the beginning of the 1990s Sallie Mae held 28 percent of all federal student loans; the next closest competitor held around 4 percent.[14] By the end of 1999 Fannie Mae and Freddie Mac owned or had securitized 47 percent of outstanding conventional (that is, not government-insured or -guaranteed) single-family mortgage loans. Fannie Mae purchased $316 billion in single-family loans in 1999, and Freddie Mac, $233 billion.[15]

TABLE 1-4
GROWTH OF FCS, 1970–2000

Year	Obligations
1970	$13.3 billion
1975	$28.1 billion
1980	$60.4 billion
1985	$70.0 billion
1990	$55.2 billion
1995	$61.5 billion
2000	$79.6 billion

SOURCE: CBO, *Controlling the Risks*, and FCS annual financial statements, 1970–2000.

TABLE 1-5
GROWTH OF SALLIE MAE, 1970–2000

Year	Obligations
1970	n.a.
1975	$0.3 billion
1980	$2.7 billion
1985	$13.4 billion
1990	$39.0 billion
1995	$47.5 billion
2000	$47.2 billion

SOURCE: CBO, *Controlling the Risks;* Sallie Mae and USA Education, Inc., annual financial statements, 1970–2000.
NOTE: Some of the 2000 borrowing may be non-GSE debt; the 2000 USA Education, Inc., financial statements are not clear on this point.

GSEs tend to be extremely profitable for their owners. The large investor-owned GSEs, Fannie Mae and Freddie Mac, have used their growth as the basis for providing substantial returns on equity to their shareholders year in and year out (table 1-6). The returns on equity are unique for consistently exceeding 20 percent, far more than the historical average returns of other financial institutions such as commercial banks or thrift institutions.

Along with growth in size each year, those two GSEs have expanded the scope of their business activities. Fannie Mae and Freddie

TABLE 1-6
RETURNS ON EQUITY, FANNIE MAE AND FREDDIE MAC, 1990–2000

Year	Fannie Mae	Freddie Mac
1990	33.7%	20.4%
1992	26.5%	21.2%
1994	24.3%	23.3%
1996	24.1%	22.6%
1998	25.2%	22.6%
2000	25.6%	23.7%

SOURCE: Office of Federal Housing Enterprise Oversight, *2001 Report to Congress* (Washington, D.C.: Government Printing Office, 2001), table 24, p. 78. Returns are on common equity.

FIGURE 1-1
THE EFFECT OF AUTOMATED UNDERWRITING ON THE
ENTERPRISES' ROLE IN THE LOAN ORIGINATION PROCESS

Traditional Role of the Enterprises in Underwriting a Loan

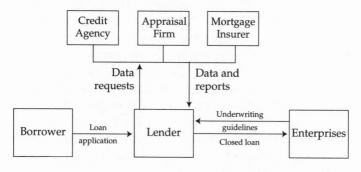

Alternative Enterprise Role Using Automated Underwriting

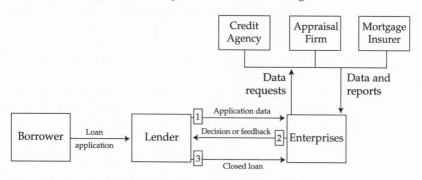

SOURCE: Office of Federal Housing Enterprise Oversight, *1995 Report to Congress* (Washington, D.C.: Government Printing Office, 1995), fig. 1, p. 4.
NOTE: Lender has the option to do business directly with appraisal firms and mortgage insurers.

Mac began to deploy automated underwriting systems in 1995 and so captured much of the value-added that lenders in the primary market, such as mortgage banks, commercial banks, and thrift institutions, had earlier provided. Figure 1-1 shows how this shift occurred. In other words the GSEs are beginning to erase the boundaries between the primary and secondary mortgage markets, at least in functional terms.[16] For example, Fannie Mae and Freddie Mac have rolled out programs, either alone or as part of a joint venture, to provide underwriting guidance for mortgage brokers,[17] as well as programs directed specifically at consumers.[18] (As discussed in chapter 4, the Federal Home Loan Bank of Chicago is also implementing a program to erase the distinction between the primary and secondary mortgage markets.)

Fannie Mae and Freddie Mac have expanded in other ways. Applying techniques of credit scoring and loan scoring to the mortgage market, the two GSEs serve a small but increasing portion of the so-called subprime home mortgage market, including borrowers of lower creditworthiness than traditionally might have qualified for a mortgage and borrowers in the home equity market. Fannie Mae has also indicated that it is becoming more active in the market that the government traditionally has served through Federal Housing Administration mortgages.[19]

As they have become financial behemoths, the three housing GSEs have become more controversial. One source of friction is a concern of policy analysts and private competitors that GSEs are expanding and profiting on the basis of their governmental benefits rather than because of the financial acumen of their managers.[20] The government rather than economic efficiency is picking the winners in the home mortgage market.

Thus, thanks to their government subsidies, Fannie Mae and Freddie Mac enjoy what a year 2000 Bernstein Research report calls "hegemony in the mortgage market." The stock analysts' report begins with the following description of the GSEs: "Fannie Mae and Freddie Mac enjoy profound competitive advantages versus all other mortgage market participants, which confer on the agencies [*sic*] virtual dominance of our largest financial market.[21]

The Congressional Budget Office frames the issue this way for the two largest GSEs:

> The popular perception of Fannie Mae and Freddie Mac as benefactors of homebuyers for whom they reduce interest rates and increase home ownership deserves examination. In fact, the housing GSEs are principally a vehicle for delivering a federal subsidy rather than the source of that subsidy. Moreover, the estimates presented suggest that they are not an efficient delivery vehicle because they retain nearly $1 for every $2 they pass through.[22]

The CBO study adds that GSEs may provide some benefits besides conveying a subsidy but such benefits are hard to value, especially because they are generally available from other, fully private firms that operate without government sponsorship. In 2001 the CBO updated its study to include the Federal Home Loan Banks. The CBO found that Fannie Mae and Freddie Mac passed on 63 percent of their government subsidies to homebuyers in 2000 and kept somewhat more of the subsidy than in 1995. The allocation of the benefits of the GSE subsidy for the Federal Home Loan Banks was even less equitable; most of the subsidy went to the banks themselves and their shareholders, with only a tiny fraction helping to lower borrowing costs for consumers.[23]

The two GSEs have imposed standardization on mortgage forms and procedures that in the 1970s helped to reduce transaction costs and improve the efficiency of mortgage origination, servicing, and funding.[24] However, standardization can be a two-edged sword. As the GSEs gained market power, the concentration of financial power in just two companies has apparently stifled competition and innovation that might otherwise have taken place. A 1999 Department of Housing and Urban Development study indicates that the two GSEs' underwriting guidelines may have the effect of limiting lending to minority borrowers.[25] The effect is compounded by the absence of other institutions that in a competitive market might apply different guidelines to purchase such loans at comparable prices. The dominance of two GSE underwriting systems can deny access to the conforming mortgage market to some borrowers who might otherwise be served if more open competition among lenders existed. The denial of access to the conforming market could drive some borrowers into doing business on unsavory terms and could deny other borrowers market access altogether.

Origins of the GSEs

The GSEs' dramatic expansion and displacement of many other competitors in the financial markets stand in contrast to their early history. Some reference to the origins and original purposes of GSEs shows how far they have come. The government began most GSEs to help overcome perceived imperfections in the credit markets.

Legislation authorized the Farm Credit System in 1916 as a way to provide credit when electricity and automobiles were uncommon in rural America and farm communities often were remote from competitive sources of credit. Proponents saw the system as "a second National Bank System."[26] The new FCS institutions could help to underwrite credit and provide funds to creditworthy rural borrowers who found themselves isolated from the financial centers of the United States and the commercial banks that served urban borrowers. By creating an alternative delivery system for credit in those communities, the FCS helped to encourage the flow of credit. FCS institutions pioneered several innovations, including self-amortizing loans, point-of-sale loans for farm equipment, variable rate loans, and lines of credit for farm borrowers.[27]

As discussed in chapter 6, the government began the Federal Home Loan Banks in 1932, in the depths of the Great Depression. Thrift industry advocates, pointing to the benefits of the Federal Reserve System for commercial banks and of the Farm Credit System for rural borrowers, asked for similar federal credit support for thrift institutions and urban areas.[28]

Fannie Mae also began in the Great Depression, in 1938. As a wholly owned government corporation subsidiary of the Reconstruction Finance Corporation, it was to help fund mortgage loans insured by another new deal agency, the Federal Housing Administration. The government enacted legislation in 1968 to convert Fannie Mae into a GSE and chartered Freddie Mac as a new GSE in 1970. Both GSEs were then authorized to provide a secondary market for conventional mortgage loans in addition to government-insured and guaranteed loans.

Legislation chartered Sallie Mae in 1972 as part of an effort to provide funding for the recently established federal student loan program. Student loans had unusual financial characteristics and were small and costly to service in small numbers. Banks tended to offer student loans to their customers primarily as a way to build consumer loyalty for other financial products. Sallie Mae offered an opportunity to create a large-scale financial institution that could purchase large volumes of student loans and develop profitable economies of scale.

By contrast to these examples, market imperfections are much more difficult to find today. Since its original authorization in 1987, Farmer Mac, the newest GSE, has had to return to Congress several times to obtain adjustments to its charter powers to offer increasingly profitable types of financial services. The GSE has not been a strong success in public policy terms.[29] Farmer Mac continues to make a large part of its earnings from financial investments that have nothing to do with meeting public needs.

Despite such shortcomings from a policy point of view, many constituencies support the further expansion of GSE activities. As Peter Wallison observes, the GSEs' ability to deliver an off-budget subsidy is politically attractive in today's legislative environment:

> As long as they are left without oversight or political restriction, their off-budget, market-based funding allows them to expand indefinitely without having to go back to Congress. In other words, favored constituency groups get benefits for which congressmen and senators can claim credit, but there is no need for new taxes or offsets that might put them into competition with other congressional priorities.[30]

The GSE as a Mercantilist Institution

As an institutional form, the private company chartered by a government to carry out public purposes has a lineage to the mercantilist period in Europe. John Weicher puts it nicely: the GSE part of today's housing finance system in the United States "has an Elizabethan character."[31] In mercantilist times, dating approximately from the sixteenth through the eighteenth centuries, the sovereign chartered private companies, such as the Bank of England and the East India Company, to carry out activities that the state could not carry out for itself.

As detailed in chapter 5, the Bank of England became Alexander Hamilton's model for the first Bank of the United States, a central bank primarily privately owned, with a one-fifth government stake, and governed by a private board of directors. The bank, chartered for twenty years, terminated in 1811. The government chartered the second Bank of the United States in 1816, again for a twenty-year period, and later chartered other private companies, notably transcontinental railroads and a system of national banks, to perform public functions. In 1913 the government created the Federal Reserve System as the nation's new central bank. Building on these antecedents and on U.S. studies of cooperative organizations in Europe, the federal government created the first GSE, the Farm Credit System. The creation of the other GSEs followed in subsequent decades.

Early chartered companies such as the English East India Company and the Bank of England added significant institutional strength as the government sought to overcome two types of institutional shortcoming prevalent in the mercantilist period. First, the government lacked the capacity to carry out many public purposes through its own administrative apparatus. Private monopolies provided a useful institutional form to carry out purposes of an entrepreneurial nature. Second, markets were undeveloped in mercantilist times. The creation of a chartered monopoly backed by the authority of the state helped to concentrate scarce resources within a single institution and apply them to the most pressing public purposes.

Today's GSEs have somewhat changed the mercantilist model. Instead of proscribing other firms from competing with a mercantilist monopoly in its designated market as government did in mercantilist times, the U.S. government has achieved a similar result by tying substantial government subsidies to the fortunes of a handful of GSEs.[32] Thanks to the government subsidy for GSEs, the marketplace has been unable to impose efficient or effective limits on the growth of most GSEs. Some GSEs—notably the Farm Credit System during a virtual agricultural depression in the 1980s and the Federal Home Loan Bank System during the thrift industry debacle—have sometimes faced significant reversals of financial fortune. For several of the GSEs, however, the availability of an open-ended federal subsidy has permitted dramatic growth and displacement of private competitors. The mercantilist model is proving to have serious shortcomings in today's environment.

With this introduction in mind, the following chapters look at the institutional characteristics of GSEs from different perspectives. Chapter 2 explores the nature of the GSE as a special kind of instrumentality of government. Chapter 3 examines the implications of the government's creation of a perception of implicit backing of GSEs and their obligations. Chapter 4 focuses on the authorized powers of GSEs under their charter acts. Chapter 5 considers the governance of GSEs and the differences in behavior between investor-owned GSEs and cooperative GSEs. Chapter 6 returns to a historical perspective on GSEs and the historical antecedents of the unusual institutions, while chapter 7 concludes with a discussion of exit strategies and current issues affecting GSEs.

2
Instrumentalities of Government

The first important design feature of the GSE is its structure as an instrumentality of the federal government. Instrumentalities are organizations that carry out public purposes but are not part of the government itself. Federal instrumentalities can be private companies, nonprofit organizations, or parts of state government that carry out public purposes under federal law. As instrumentalities of government, the six privately owned GSEs occupy a middle ground on the organizational continuum between government agencies and wholly private companies.

An understanding of the legal aspects of instrumentality status can help to alleviate some confusion about GSEs regarding their mixture of governmental and private attributes. This chapter looks first at instrumentalities generally and then at the instrumentality status of GSEs in particular.

Unusual Legal Attributes of Federal Instrumentalities

Types of Federal Instrumentality. Instrumentalities of the federal government include institutions that (1) Congress charters directly through authorizing legislation, (2) Congress authorizes a federal regulator to charter, and (3) a state charters and then gains status as a federal instrumentality from the enactment of federal law.

Early examples of instrumentalities chartered directly by Congress include the two Banks of the United States and the Union Pacific Railroad Company. Current examples include several GSEs—Fannie Mae, Freddie Mac, and Sallie Mae—and a number of nonprofit organizations such as the American National Red Cross.

Examples of institutions that federal regulators charter as instrumentalities include national banks, federal savings and loan associations (that is, thrift institutions), and federal credit unions. Regulators also charter some GSEs, notably the institutions of the Farm Credit System and the Federal Home Loan Bank System.

Federal law can also confer instrumentality status on an organization chartered under the laws of a state. State-chartered commercial banks and thrift institutions acquire the status of federal instrumentalities, at least for some purposes, when they receive federal deposit insurance.[1] Before the establishment of federal deposit insurance, state-chartered commercial banks became federal instrumentalities for some purposes when they joined the Federal Reserve System.[2] State governments also can create instrumentalities. State instrumentalities may include some private utilities, hospitals, insurance companies, and other organizations designated to serve a special public purpose. Nonprofit organizations are special forms of federal or state instrumentality, and the nonprofit authority is an important subset of these nonprofit instrumentalities.[3] Table 2-1 provides an overview of today's federal and state instrumentalities. Although these are only examples, many instrumentalities are intended to provide financial services.

Attributes. The courts have long acknowledged the federal government's authority to use private institutions to serve public purposes. In *Osborn v. Bank of the United States*, Chief Justice John Marshall explained the role of the Bank of the United States as a federal instrumentality: "The bank is not considered as a private corporation, whose principal object is individual trade and individual profit; but as a public corporation, created for public and national purposes. . . . The bank is an instrument which is 'necessary and proper for carrying into effect the powers vested in the government of the United States.'"[4]

Service to public purposes distinguishes the instrumentality of the government from other private firms and organizations. Under the applicable legislation, the government has several ways to help ensure that instrumentalities serve public purposes. Those include provisions limiting the scope of authorized powers that an instrumentality may carry out, governance or organizational requirements, and government oversight of the activities that instrumentalities carry out under their enabling legislation.

Table 2-2 lists some ways that government may use to try to promote accountability of GSEs and other instrumentalities. The ef-

TABLE 2-1
FEDERAL AND STATE INSTRUMENTALITIES TODAY

	Federally Chartered	State-Chartered
Financial services institutions	Federal Reserve Banks; national banks; most thrift institutions; most credit unions; Securities Investor Protection Corporation; six GSEs	Commercial banks; some thrift institutions; some credit unions; insurance companies; nonprofit state finance authorities (for example, housing, student loans, development)
Other companies and nonprofits	Comsat; American National Red Cross; National Park Foundation	Public authorities and some utilities; hospitals; municipal corporations

fectiveness of those approaches varies according to the political influence that a particular instrumentality wields, as well as economic factors that may affect the incentive of an instrumentality to serve public purposes along with its own private interests.

By itself the enactment of federal legislation to charter an institution does not confer instrumentality status.[5] The federal government has also chartered private corporations. However, unless they serve public purposes under law, such corporations are not instrumentalities. For example, the National Consumer Cooperative Bank operates under a federal charter and with the benefit of a long-term low-interest federal loan. Although it began as an instrumentality of the United States, subsequent legislation transformed the bank into "a federally chartered private bank owned and controlled by its cooperative stockholders."[6] Today the bank raises money in the private debt markets and funds large and profitable cooperatives without regard to public purposes.

Among federally chartered nonprofit organizations, the American National Red Cross is a federal instrumentality.[7] It helps to carry out treaty obligations of the United States under the Geneva conventions. By contrast many other congressionally chartered nonprofit organizations are not federal instrumentalities, even though they serve educational, charitable, or similar functions.[8]

Comparison with the Government Agency. There is some confusion between instrumentalities and agencies of government. The

TABLE 2-2
PROMOTING ACCOUNTABILITY OF
PRIVATE INSTITUTIONS TO PUBLIC PURPOSES

Charter Act Limitations on Authorized Powers	Governance-Organization Requirements	Supervision by a Government Agency
Specification of permitted functions	Inclusion of directors appointed by government	Oversight and regulation of activities
Limited new market segments	Inclusion of directors to represent particular	Required approval of activities
Restricted members or customers	constituencies	Supervision of safety and soundness
Requirement to serve designated market segments	Specification of investor or cooperative or nonprofit structure	

distinction deserves clarification. An *instrumentality* carries out public purposes without being a part of government. Instrumentalities such as commercial banks, thrift institutions, and GSEs are private companies that carry out public purposes under the terms of some federal law.

As private firms, those instrumentalities of government are not covered by the many laws that apply to government agencies. The directors and officers and employees of instrumentalities do not become officers or employees of the United States as a result of holding their private positions.[9] Instrumentalities are generally exempt from the many restrictions on resources, staffing, procurement, and procedures that apply to federal agencies. Even though an instrumentality carries out public purposes, its actions do not usually constitute "state action" for purposes of those restrictions that the Constitution imposes on the government of the United States. Finally, instrumentalities do not benefit from the sovereign immunity of the government, even though they carry out public purposes under law.[10]

By contrast a *federal agency* is a part of the federal government. Public officials control and manage federal agencies. The officials and employees of a federal agency are officers and employees of the United States. With some variations, federal agencies are subject to a plethora of federal laws, especially relating to management, that do not apply to the private sector or to instrumentalities of government. Federal laws applicable to agencies include the Administrative Procedure Act, Freedom of Information Act, Sunshine Act, Privacy Act, federal civil service and classification laws, federal budget laws, and procurement laws.[11]

The *government-owned corporation* deserves mention as a special type of government agency. The federal government uses government corporations such as the Tennessee Valley Authority or the U.S. Postal Service, with some significant variations, to administer government programs and activities that are revenue producing and potentially self-sustaining. The organizational form, owned and managed by government, carries out its functions as a legally distinct entity within the government. The government corporation differs from the traditional government agency in the nature of the government controls, budget treatment, and other attributes that may apply, all with variations.

Depending on their methods of operation and especially on the extent that they are held responsible for meeting performance-based standards and a financial bottom line rather than being controlled by traditional governmental input controls over budget, staffing and other resources, such government corporations may exhibit superior management to many other government agencies.[12] The Government Corporation Control Act of 1945[13] distinguishes two types of government corporation: the *wholly owned government corporation* (for example, Ginnie Mae, the Government National Mortgage Association) and the so-called *mixed-ownership government corporation* (for example, the Federal Deposit Insurance Corporation).

Until 1954 Fannie Mae was a wholly owned government corporation. That year, in response to pressure to remove the corporation from the federal budget, the Eisenhower administration converted Fannie Mae to a so-called mixed ownership corporation. In 1968, again in response to budget pressures,[14] the government enacted legislation to convert Fannie Mae to a privately owned GSE.

In organizational terms the difference between government agencies and instrumentalities of government generally follows the fundamental distinction between public and private sector institutions. The government directly manages a government agency; by contrast the government may merely supervise an instrumentality through regulation and oversight from outside the organization. Private owners and managers actually operate the instrumentality.

Despite the importance of the difference, the terms *agency* and *instrumentality* have been confused in some judicial decisions and in general parlance. Part of the confusion may be traced to the decision of the Supreme Court in *Smith v. Kansas City Title & Trust Co.*,[15] which held that Congress was within its constitutional powers to create the federal land banks, early FCS institutions. That case based constitutionality of the 1916 Federal Farm Loan Act on the authority of Congress to create the land banks and give them statutory authority to act as fiscal and financial agents of the federal government; subsequent cases seem to have confused the concept of federal *agents* with federal *agencies*.

The practice of financial analysts to designate instrumentalities of the federal government as agencies rather than instrumentalities also confuses the nomenclature in the area. GSEs borrow in the so-called federal agency credit market, along with government agencies such as the Tennessee Valley Authority. The financial markets concern themselves with the perceived governmental backing of obligations of such organizations, rather than whether the organizations are agencies of government in the legal and public administration sense of the term.[16]

Comparison with the Ordinary Private Company. U.S. law of corporations is a marvel of institutional design. Private companies may incorporate under the laws of a state with little difficulty. The law sets forth the rights and responsibilities of corporation owners and managers and creates enforceable duties such as the fiduciary responsibility of managers to protect the interests of the company and its shareholders. The corporation law of a state permits the general-purpose private company to engage in any lines of business unless a specific statutory provision prohibits a particular business activity. The usual private company has considerable latitude to develop business strategies and to enter and leave lines of business as it finds appropriate. If a company is successful, it grows; if it fails financially, its creditors may throw it into bankruptcy and put it out of business.

Similar to the ordinary private company, private shareholders may own and control an instrumentality. However, the instrumentality operates within a completely different legal framework. First, as explored in chapter 4, the federal government charters or otherwise shapes the activities of instrumentalities under authorizing legislation similar to the laws that authorize government agencies to engage in their statutory activities. In that way government can seek to direct the activities of federal instrumentalities to serve public purposes.

Banks, thrift institutions, credit unions, and GSEs are particular types of instrumentalities of government. As instrumentalities, they operate under laws that limit their activities to those that embody a public purpose. The public purpose of a federal instrumentality is defined by the terms of its charter act or other federal law that endows the organization with instrumentality status. National banks were established "to provide a uniform and secure currency for the people, and to facilitate the operations of the Treasury of the United States."[17] Thrift institutions have a statutory public purpose of providing "for the deposit or investment of funds and for the extension of credit for homes and other goods and services."[18] A credit union is chartered "for the purpose of promoting thrift among its members and creating a source of credit for provident or productive purposes."[19]

Enabling legislation similarly sets forth the public purposes of each government-sponsored enterprise. Summarizing the original public purposes of the GSEs, the General Accounting Office states that the federal government established the GSEs "because it wanted to ensure that reasonably priced credit was available for borrowers seeking to finance homes, agricultural businesses, and college education.... The GSEs were created to correct what were perceived as flaws in the credit markets."[20] In general terms Fannie Mae and Freddie Mac provide a secondary market for residential mortgages, Sallie Mae funds student loans, the Federal Home Loan Banks provide credit for their member institutions, and the Farm Credit System and Farmer Mac provide credit to agricultural borrowers and rural borrowers.

A second important legal attribute of federal instrumentalities is the preemption by federal law of state law in important respects. Federal law may preempt state law with respect to the taxation of an instrumentality. This legal principle traces to Chief Justice John Marshall and the case of *McCulloch v. Maryland*,[21] involving the second Bank of the United States. Federal law determines the extent that a state may tax a particular instrumentality, if at all.

Federal law may preempt state laws that require registration or licensure before doing business in the state or that attempt to apply special rules to particular transactions such as foreclosure. Unlike a state-chartered bank or insurance company, a federal instrumentality generally need not register or obtain a license in the states where it may do business. Federal law may also preempt laws that the states might enact to protect consumers, such as state usury laws. Federal criminal laws often apply to persons who commit crimes against an instrumentality.[22] The courts justify the preemption on the grounds that the federal government has the constitutional authority to use criminal laws to help protect the instrumentalities that it properly creates or uses for public purposes. In such cases federal and state laws may apply to the same criminal act.

Third, besides imposing accountability on an instrumentality to undertake lines of business to serve public purposes, as discussed in chapter 4, the law may provide special benefits. The government provides such benefits to help support the public purposes that the instrumentality is to serve. Congress has been quite flexible in the choice of special privileges that the law confers on different kinds of instrumentalities. Commercial banks receive access to the check-clearing process of the Federal Reserve System and deposit insurance; credit unions receive special tax exemptions and deposit insurance; and thrift institutions receive deposit insurance.

GSEs receive tax and regulatory exemptions, which vary from GSE to GSE. They also receive a distinctive benefit from the perception that the federal government stands behind their financial obligations. The unique attribute means that GSEs fund themselves on favorable terms in the federal agency credit market, as discussed in chapter 3.

Public Purposes

Congress was able to specify valuable public purposes when it created some of the earlier GSEs. As discussed in chapter 1, the public purposes involved the provision of government-backed credit to overcome imperfections in the credit markets. The evolution of highly efficient financial markets in the United States has meant that most of the original market imperfections no longer exist. Today the value of many GSEs appears to be their utility as vehicles for delivering an off-budget government subsidy to favored constituencies in housing, agriculture, and education.

As a general rule, the government can use three approaches to try to ensure that GSEs serve high-priority public purposes throughout their existence. First, the government can try to define the authorized activities of a GSE with some specificity and then adjust the statutory provisions over time. The approach is limited by (1) the government's inability to muster the political will to make a GSE give up any part of its asserted charter act authority, (2) the lack of understanding among policymakers of the consequences of making particular changes in a GSE's enabling legislation, and (3) the tendency of Congress to enact small so-called technical amendments that the GSEs propose, again without a full airing of how the legislation will relax previous limitations that directed a GSE to serve particular public purposes in a particular way.

Second, the government can vest a government department or agency with the authority to require service to particular public purposes within the framework of the GSE's charter act. Thus, as elaborated in chapter 6, the law directs the secretary of housing and urban development to establish goals for Fannie Mae and Freddie Mac to fund mortgages for underserved borrowers and communities. However, the law states that when funding mortgages for low- and moderate-income housing, the GSEs are supposed to receive a "reasonable economic return that may be less than the return earned on other activities." That limitation, plus the relative political weakness of the Department of Housing and Urban Development vis-à-vis the GSEs, has meant that the department's housing goals do not require the GSEs to do more to serve underserved borrowers (for example, minorities or lower-income borrowers or communities) than other mortgage market lenders already do.[23]

Trying to implement such goals is a structural problem. June O'Neill, then director of the Congressional Budget Office, explained the problem.

> Of course we have food stamps. But suppose instead that we said the way we are going to provide subsidized food to low income people in the District of Columbia is to give a subsidy to Giant and Safeway [the two dominant food retailers] and expect them to pass it on. Well, they would be in a quandary. They would be getting this subsidy that would enable them to be more profitable. What would they do with it?. . . I think everyone would easily see that is an inefficient thing to do.
>
> That is sort of what we have been doing with Fannie Mae and Freddie Mac in terms of requiring them to do additional good deeds and try to subsidize low income populations.[24]

Third, and potentially most effective, the government can simply require that a GSE set aside a fixed percentage of its income to serve high-priority public purposes. In 1989 Congress amended the Federal Home Loan Bank Act to require that the Federal Home Loan Banks set aside 10 percent of their income each year in a fund to help reduce the costs of mortgages for underserved borrowers and communities. The Federal Housing Finance Board, the government regulator of the federal home loan banks, oversees this affordable housing fund. The value of the approach is the limitations on the ability of a GSE to use its political strength against a regulator to reduce the amount of its contribution to meeting the needs specified by law. The percentage of income is fixed by law and thus is easier for the government to administer.

Legal Attributes

On the one hand, because of their private ownership and private control, the six GSEs share many attributes of private companies. The stock of investor-owned GSEs trades on the New York Stock Exchange and is followed closely by equity analysts of the major investment banking houses. GSE officers and employees earn compensation comparable to that of other financial institutions of similar size, often including compensation based on the appreciation in price of a GSE's stock. The investor-owned GSEs pay federal income taxes as private companies, and all GSEs publish audited financial statements according to the generally acceptable accounting principles (GAAP) that apply to private companies.

GSEs may sue and be sued in court as private companies and generally do not benefit from sovereign immunity.[25] Actions of a GSE do not amount to state action for purposes of constitutional limitations that apply to the federal government.[26] Their employees are not officers or employees of the federal government. The GSEs are not agencies of the United States for purposes of the many laws that apply to the federal government, such as the Freedom of Information Act or federal civil service or procurement or budget laws.

On the other hand, the six GSEs share some characteristics with government agencies. They borrow money in a manner that allows the markets to infer that they are backed by the government (even though the law and their offering circulars specifically state otherwise). Federal law also provides them special regulatory and tax benefits unavailable to other private companies. With some variations

- their securities are deemed exempt securities under the laws administered by the Securities and Exchange Commission and thus are exempt from SEC registration;
- they are generally exempt from state and local income taxation;
- the Federal Home Loan Banks and parts of the Farm Credit System are exempt from federal income taxes[27]; and
- interest on obligations of the Federal Home Loan Bank System, the Farm Credit System, and Sallie Mae is exempt from state income taxation.

As instrumentalities, GSEs operate on the basis of authorizing legislation that prescribes the extent of their permitted activities. Their enabling legislation seeks to specify the market segments and types of customer that each GSE may serve and the goods and services that it may provide. In contrast to ordinary private companies, GSEs may engage only in those activities that they are expressly authorized to carry out or that are incidental to their otherwise authorized activities. Chapter 4 explores that aspect.

Because of their special benefits and government subsidies, the law tends to favor GSEs in their competition with other firms. The law provides the GSEs with a number of benefits that are unavailable to other instrumentalities or ordinary private companies:

- Unlike banks or thrift institutions, GSEs each hold a unique legal charter. The charter creates barriers that help protect the GSE against the possibility that a new entrant will benefit from the same system of statutory privileges.
- Federal law typically authorizes GSEs to operate with less capital and higher financial leverage than required of other firms in similar lines of business—a significant competitive advantage.
- Access to the agency credit market allows GSEs to borrow huge amounts of money at less cost than is available to competitors. The combination of high leverage and low borrowing costs has allowed the larger GSEs to grow into much larger institutions than otherwise would be likely.
- Exemption from jurisdiction of the Securities and Exchange Commission and exemption from state and local income taxes (and for the Farm Credit System and Federal Home Loan Bank System, from federal income taxes) adds to the competitive advantage over other firms.

Robert Van Order, chief economist of Freddie Mac, has pointed out the consequences of the variation in special government privileges for different instrumentalities. When GSEs compete with banks, thrift institutions, or other firms, the variation in the types of benefits creates a system of what he calls "dueling charters."[28] The result is not economically superior: to the extent that particular instrumentalities rather than ordinary private companies dominate a market, that market reflects the model from mercantilist times, when entrepreneurs with the most favorable charters, rather than the most efficient companies, captured the relevant market and made the most money.

Similar to government agencies, GSEs possess federal charters that generally preempt state laws in their operations, including state and local income tax laws and also state doing-business laws that otherwise could require a GSE to license or register with state authorities to do business in the state. GSEs also benefit from court decisions that deem some of their business activities to involve a federal interest and thus to preempt state laws.[29]

Table 2-3 presents an overview of the legal characteristics of GSEs compared with ordinary private companies on the one hand and with government agencies on the other. GSEs differ from ordinary private companies because their creation, the permitted activities, and the exit of failed GSEs are shaped by law and governmental actions rather than the marketplace. In contrast to government agencies, conversely, GSEs are not part of the government. With some exceptions that are disappearing over time, they are not generally subject to government control of their budgets, staffing, and internal corporate affairs.

Institutional Characteristics

The legal characteristics of GSEs have significant consequences for their operating environment, accountability, incentives, and life cycles.

Operating Environment. Unlike the ordinary private company but like the government agency, the GSE lives or dies according to the value of the benefits provided by its enabling legislation. The significance of the benefits gives the GSE considerable incentive to address political issues that affect its charter, not merely the economic aspects of its market. When market conditions made service to its

TABLE 2-3
LEGAL ATTRIBUTES OF GSEs COMPARED WITH
ORDINARY PRIVATE COMPANIES AND GOVERNMENT AGENCIES

Ordinary Company	Government-Sponsored Enterprise	Government Agency
Organized under generally applicable laws to serve private purposes	Organized to serve public purposes; considered an instrumentality of government; federal charter preempts state taxes and laws	Organized as a part of the government to serve public purposes; federal law preempts state taxes and laws
Organized as a legally distinct entity	Organized as a legally distinct entity	Generally part of government, administratively and for budget purposes; the government corporation is a legally distinct entity
Can usually obtain a license to do business by registering with a government department	Created by specific authority of law; must obtain a charter (1) from Congress or (2) from a federal regulatory agency according to statutory standards	Created by specific authority of law
Authorized to conduct general business activities except as expressly prohibited by law	Authorized to conduct only those activities expressly permitted by law	Authorized to conduct only those activities expressly permitted by law
Can freely enter lines of business except where entry is prohibited by laws; can freely stop serving markets or customers	Can enter only lines of business authorized by law; may be required to serve particular markets or customers	Can provide only services authorized by law; may be required to provide particular types of service

(Table continues on the following page.)

TABLE 2-3
(*continued*)

Ordinary Company	Government-Sponsored Enterprise	Government Agency
Generally has no unique benefits granted by law; often operates in contested markets	Has unique benefits granted by law to a single GSE or group of GSEs; often protected by law from entry by competitors; often has market power or even monopoly power	Has special benefits granted by law and sovereign privileges and immunities unless expressly waived by law (for example, government corporations); may be a monopolist in the provision of public goods and services
Often unregulated	Somewhat regulated, for example, with respect to permitted lines of business	Usually controlled through executive branch procedures, for example, with respect to budget, staffing, or procurement
Can be forced into bankruptcy by unsatisfied creditors	Probably cannot be forced into bankruptcy, even if insolvent; must be terminated by government action	Generally has sovereign immunity from bankruptcy; can be terminated only by law

authorized markets unattractive, Farmer Mac, the newest GSE, returned to Congress on several occasions to expand its charter authority. At some point the combination of federal tax and other subsidy benefits can make virtually any GSE a remunerative venture for its owners.

Like the ordinary private company but unlike the government agency, the GSE is not limited by law or by resource constraints from dedicating considerable resources to mastering its political environment. The need to master the political environment, plus access to ample financial resources, makes the GSEs formidable players in the legislative and regulatory processes of the federal government.

Institutional Capacity. As a privately owned institution, the GSE can benefit from access to resources that permit the development of substantial institutional capacity. Fannie Mae and Freddie Mac can use their revenues to employ 3,900 and 3,700 people, respectively, plus many contractors. They can offer generous compensation packages to retain people with technical and financial skills. Investor-owned GSEs can offer stock options of extraordinary value to their directors, officers, and employees.

In that respect the investor-owned GSE appears superior to the cooperative GSE. The positions taken by its members constrain a cooperative GSE in many ways (chapter 6 explores this topic). The attitudes of members can keep compensation levels down, as the Farm Credit System experienced in the years before its financial failure in 1985. Although the system appears to have been overstaffed, the outlook of borrower-members of most FCS institutions seemed to be that compensation of FCS officials should be judged according to farmer incomes rather the need to retain services of qualified financial professionals. In the aftermath of the FCS failure and with the need to ensure the hiring and retention of high-quality officials, the system increased compensation to more competitive levels.

As private institutions, GSEs can build significantly greater institutional capacity than many government agencies. Although the comparison is not totally appropriate, the capacity of Fannie Mae and Freddie Mac contrasts starkly with the capable but understaffed Ginnie Mae, a wholly owned government corporation that also serves the secondary mortgage market. In contrast to the thousands of employees at the two GSEs, Ginnie Mae has found itself hampered in its efforts to hire appropriate personnel and maintain staffing at levels around sixty-five full-time employees to manage an outstanding portfolio of guaranteed mortgage-backed securities amounting to more than half a trillion dollars. Compensation for those employees—at federal civil service levels—also lags GSE compensation levels by significant amounts.[30]

Accountability and Incentives. Like the ordinary private company and unlike the government agency, the directors and officers of a GSE have a fiduciary responsibility to the company and its owners. That responsibility holds for both investor-owned GSEs and the GSEs that are structured to be cooperative in form. The government-appointed directors of a GSE have the same fiduciary obligation.[31]

Accountability to shareholders means that GSEs must disclose material information about the business. Although GSE charter acts generally exempt GSE securities from the jurisdiction of the Securities and Exchange Commission, the GSEs are subject to antifraud provisions of the securities laws. The rights of shareholders in an investor-owned GSE and of investors in other GSE securities are somewhat less certain than the rights of investors in the securities of the ordinary private corporation. Part of the problem relates to the lack of a federal corporation law that would define the rights of shareholders and bondholders vis-à-vis the GSE and its managers.[32]

To a varying extent GSEs also are accountable to a federal regulator. Federal regulators may supervise the financial safety and soundness of a GSE or its service to public purposes or both. GSE regulators generally do not have the authority to intervene in the internal corporate affairs of a GSE except in relation to safety and soundness. The two regulators of multimember GSEs, the Farm Credit Administration (vis-à-vis the Farm Credit System) and the Federal Housing Finance Board (vis-à-vis the Federal Home Loan Bank System), have the authority to charter individual institutions within the GSE system.

As detailed later, the officers and directors of GSEs perceive themselves as owing their primary allegiance to shareholders rather than to the federal government that charters them. As the president and CEO of Sallie Mae, Edward A. Fox, once told a Senate subcommittee: "We are a private corporation and as such, with stockholders and bondholders, we have a fiduciary responsibility to those individuals. . . . We are not charged with subsidizing the guaranteed student loan program or subsidizing the students."[33]

In other words the government charters a GSE with the idea of using the incentive structure of a private institution to achieve public purposes. As in a private company, the interests of the private owners come first in the minds of company directors and officers. Unlike the ordinary private company and much as a regulated utility, service to public purposes results from the laws and regulations that the government uses to ensure that the institution serves public interests as well as private ones.[34] (Chapter 6 discusses the significant tension between private profits and the public purposes that the GSEs are supposed to serve.)

Life Cycle. The free market system enables private companies to build their businesses, grow, and prosper. If a business fails to meet the needs of its customers, other firms readily fill the gap. The competitive marketplace is a dynamic setting in which firms emerge, grow, adapt their lines of business, and sometimes fail.

The GSE has a different life cycle from the ordinary private company. At start-up the GSE often benefits from federal support. When the government created Fannie Mae as a GSE in 1968, the new private company took over a business that the government had already developed during the years when Fannie Mae had been a wholly owned government corporation. (Chapter 5 details the history.) Sallie Mae started in 1973 as an entirely new business. The GSE used a special provision of its charter act to take out a $200 million government-guaranteed loan to begin operations even before the company had issued stock to private investors.[35] Such a government benefit is generally not available to a private start-up company.

Despite the statutory advantages, establishing some GSEs and putting them on firm financial ground can be hard. The government established the Farm Credit System (FCS) in 1916 to provide an accessible source of credit for farmers. Parts of the FCS failed shortly after its inception because of a depression in rural agriculture in the 1920s. After the Great Depression began, the government supported the rural economy with a massive infusion of direct loans and loan guarantees through the Reconstruction Finance Corporation and the Federal Farm Mortgage Corporation, both wholly owned government corporations. The government provided a direct infusion of capital to the twelve Federal Land Banks of the FCS; the government's stock was completely retired only in 1968. It also took effort to establish Sallie Mae as a GSE after 1972. The managers of Sallie Mae worked hard for several years to generate interest among schools and banks to purchase stock in the GSE.

Once a GSE has established itself, a process of growth begins. The speed of growth depends on the market that the GSE is authorized to serve and the GSE's relative advantages compared with other firms in the same market. The major GSEs—Fannie Mae, Freddie Mac, the Federal Home Loan Banks, Sallie Mae, and, until the disastrous experience of the 1980s, the Farm Credit System—all have grown rapidly. The newest GSE, Farmer Mac, has had trouble establishing itself in a cyclical rural market already served by another GSE, the Farm Credit System, and by rural commercial banks. For the GSEs that have special advantages in the right market, growth can mean eventual domination of a market.

Because of the perception of government backing, GSEs do not go out of business even when they are inefficient or unsuccessful. Unlike the ordinary private company, the end stages of a GSE's life cycle can include stagnation. A GSE can use its government backing to stay afloat even if it adds little value to the overall economy. Many GSEs use the benefit of access to inexpensive federally subsidized borrowing to grow large portfolios that have little relationship to public purposes. The Federal Home Loan Banks especially, despite their growth and substantial size, use much of their borrowing to fund nonmortgage investments rather than the advances to members that were supposed to be their major financial product.

As discussed in chapter 3, the perception of government backing of GSE obligations greatly attenuates the market discipline that applies to other private companies. Similar to the consequences of federal deposit insurance for commercial banks and thrift institutions, the implicit federal backing of GSE obligations creates significant financial risk. Even when a GSE fails financially, government backing may let the institution borrow money to stay alive.

A great strength of the free market is the way that it deals with firms that fail. When a firm becomes troubled, lenders first charge more to lend it money; at some point they refuse to fund a failing firm at any price. Lacking profits and without access to borrowed funds, a failing firm soon goes out of business. From the perspective of the struggling entrepreneur, the free market can seem to be a harsh and unforgiving environment. Yet, from the perspective of the economy as a whole, the rapid demise of unsuccessful firms is an effective way to take the resources from those firms and reallocate them to more productive purposes. Economies that fail to do so can perpetuate losing economic activities that in their extreme form can sap the vitality from the whole economy.[36]

The GSE does not face such a harsh or unforgiving environment. In contrast to the ordinary private firm, the GSE can use its implicit government backing to borrow money inexpensively. In contrast to the ordinary private company, the GSE does not necessarily go out of business when it fails; GSEs do not appear to be subject to involuntary bankruptcy and instead must be closed by action of the government.[37]

When Fannie Mae was financially troubled in the early 1980s, the government responded with support, including the enactment of a special income tax break for it. Fannie Mae used its access to government-backed credit to grow its business rapidly as a way of diminishing the burden of its huge underwater portfolio. Fannie Mae's regulator, the Department of Housing and Urban Development, later reported:

> The incentive for risk-taking introduced by agency status becomes all the more powerful when the firm is experiencing financial difficulties such as FNMA and the thrifts did in the early 1980s.... FNMA's new management responded to insolvency by trying to generate new income through growth and risk-taking. [38]

Similarly, when the Farm Credit System announced in 1985 that it could not meet its obligations, the government created a new off-budget federal organization, the Farm Credit System Assistance Corporation, to funnel federally backed funds to the FCS.[39]

Table 2-4 presents a summary of some implications of the legal characteristics of GSEs, again compared with ordinary private companies and government agencies, for the environment, accountability, incentives, and life cycles of the three types of institution.

TABLE 2-4
INSTITUTIONAL CONSEQUENCES OF THE LEGAL ATTRIBUTES
OF GSEs COMPARED WITH ORDINARY PRIVATE COMPANIES
AND GOVERNMENT AGENCIES

Ordinary Company	Government-Sponsored Enterprise	Government Agency
External environment is more market-based than political.	External environment includes the market, but political factors tend to dominate.	Political factors predominate; the market affects some government corporations.
Stream of profits generates needed resources to build capacity.	Stream of profits and federal subsidies generates needed resources to build capacity.	Subject to controls on resources that often include annual appropriations limits; a tendency exists to maintain agency functions despite inadequate resources or capacity.
Accountable to private owners.	Accountable to private owners; often regulated by government as well.	Accountable to multiple parts of government and to influential constituencies.

(Table continues on the following page.)

TABLE 2-4
(*continued*)

Ordinary Company	Government-Sponsored Enterprise	Government Agency
Financial disclosure to private owners; if a publicly held firm, public disclosures also required.	Financial disclosure (less than for the ordinary company) to private owners and possibly to government regulators.	Some public disclosure; often less financial disclosure than is required for private firms.
Market-based external controls based upon financial performance.	Market-based external controls may be offset by federal subsidies; some regulatory controls.	Heavy controls on inputs (for example, budget and staffing) and procedures; government corporations may have greater autonomy.
Profit-oriented goals often force focus upon particular activities, market segments, and strategies.	Mix of profit-oriented goals and regulated service; cooperatives serve their members.	Diffuse political pressures lead to serving multiple purposes that often may not be articulated.
Life cycle: thrives or goes out of business; forced exit of failed firms.	Some GSEs have government backing at start-up; at its prime, GSE often has monopoly or market power; may stagnate over time; government backing can forestall easy exit.	Tends to stagnate over time, as public priorities change, without ceasing to exist.

3
Government Support of GSEs

GSEs receive a number of statutory benefits that are not available to ordinary private companies. Perhaps most important, the law permits GSEs to issue obligations that have many attributes of federal obligations. The market infers from those attributes and other statutory provisions of the GSE charters that the government implicitly backs GSE obligations and that the government would not let investors in these obligations take a loss should a GSE fail to meet them.

The perception of implicit government backing is the defining characteristic of the GSE as a special type of instrumentality of government. The federal government has not yet managed to deal with the consequences of the perceived implicit guarantee and the financial risk that it causes for taxpayers. Instead the government made modest reforms after one crisis, the financial failure of the Farm Credit System in the mid-1980s, and another near-crisis, the near-failure of Fannie Mae in the early 1980s, without establishing an adequate institutional infrastructure to protect taxpayers from the financial exposure that GSEs create.

Implicit Federal Backing of GSE Obligations and MBSs

Table 3-1 lists some of the major statutory provisions that give rise to the perception of government backing of GSEs and their obligations.[1] As a result of those attributes, which vary from GSE to GSE, GSE debt obligations trade in the so-called agency credit market, along with federal government securities that are backed by the full faith and credit of the federal government.[2]

TABLE 3-1
ATTRIBUTES OF GSEs AND THEIR OBLIGATIONS CONTRIBUTING
TO A PERCEPTION OF IMPLICIT GOVERNMENT BACKING

Attributes of GSEs	Attributes of GSE Obligations
Chartered by the federal government.	Treasury may approve their issuance.
Boards of directors include a minority of members appointed by government.	Eligible for Federal Reserve open market purchases.
Treasury is authorized to lend them money up to amounts specified in law (so-called Treasury backstop).	Eligible to collateralize public deposits.
	Exempt from SEC registration.
May use the Federal Reserve as fiscal agent.	Deemed government securities for purposes of the Securities Exchange Act of 1934.
Subject to audit by General Accounting Office.	Eligible for unlimited investment by federally insured banks and other depository institutions.

NOTE: Slight variations exist among GSEs. For example, the Farm Credit System does not benefit from a Treasury "backstop," does not have public directors on the boards of FCS institutions, and obtains approval from the Farm Credit Administration rather than the Treasury for the issuance of FCS consolidated obligations.

Not all those attributes are essential to the perception. For example, three federal agencies, the Federal Reserve Board, the Treasury, and the Securities and Exchange Commission (SEC), have recommended that the GSEs should lose the exemption of their securities from laws administered by the SEC, presumably in the belief that the change would not affect the perception of the government's backing.[3] Several other special benefits for GSEs, such as an exemption from state and local income taxes, do not appear to relate to the perception of the government's implicit backing.

Two GSEs, Fannie Mae and Freddie Mac, are authorized to issue mortgage-backed securities (MBSs), and their MBSs also share these agency attributes. As a consequence, Fannie Mae and Freddie

Mac MBSs trade at spreads close to MBSs that are backed by a full faith-and-credit guarantee of Ginnie Mae, a wholly owned U.S. government corporation. Farmer Mac is authorized to guarantee pools of agricultural mortgages.

One more statutory feature deserves mention. Each GSE is required to provide a disclaimer about each of its obligations. The Fannie Mae charter act contains the following provision:

> The corporation shall insert appropriate language in all of its obligations . . . clearly indicating that such obligations, together with the interest thereon, are not guaranteed by the United States and do not constitute a debt or obligation of the United States or of any agency or instrumentality thereof other than the corporation.[4]

In a perverse sort of way, the disclaimer too can be seen to hint at the perception of an *implicit* federal guarantee. The provision's technical language merely disavows an explicit government guarantee and preserves the government's option not to make good on its moral obligation. Conversely a completely private company without government sponsorship does not need any such disclaimer in its obligations. The disclaimer is part of the package of attributes applicable to GSE obligations in the agency credit market.

The GSEs themselves take great care to nurture the perception of government backing. Fannie Mae wrote to the Office of the Comptroller of the Currency to urge that GSE obligations receive even more favorable status—in terms of the amount of capital that banks should set aside to back those holdings—than the highest-rated AAA private asset-backed securities. Fannie Mae argued that "Fannie Mae standard domestic obligations, like Treasuries, typically receive no rating on an issue-by-issue basis, *because investors and rating agencies view the implied government backing of Fannie Mae as sufficient indication of the investment quality of Fannie Mae obligations*"[5] (emphasis added).

The GSEs also react vigorously if government officials suggest that the ties of GSEs to the government might be loosened. On March 22, 2000, Treasury Undersecretary Gary Gensler testified at a congressional hearing in support of legislation that would remove the ability to borrow from the Treasury, the so-called Treasury backstop, from Fannie Mae and Freddie Mac. Fannie Mae's borrowing costs increased in response to those remarks. A Fannie Mae spokesman charged that "it's unfortunate and regrettable when statements made by the Treasury have such an immediate and pronounced effect on American consumers.... The rise in mortgage costs caused by Treasury's remarks means that about 206,000 families will be disqualified for home loans."[6] Fannie Mae later apologized for the accusation and withdrew its charge that 206,000 homeowners would be priced out of the market.[7]

Even though the implicit obligation is implicit, it is real. The government faces the problem that some GSEs may be too big to fail. The issue, familiar from government rescues of other financial institutions, relates to concerns about systemic risk and the fear of policymakers that the failure of a single large institution could cause a series of failures in other institutions.[8] The reluctance of senior political officials to take the responsibility for closing a large failed institution can be especially pronounced if taxpayer money is required to pay off investors in an institution's obligations, such as federally insured depositors in failed thrift institutions in the 1980s, who relied on the implicit backing of government.

With GSEs the government faces a compounded too-big-to-fail problem. Some GSEs, with hundreds of billions or even a trillion dollars of obligations and MBSs outstanding, individually may be too big to fail. Yet, because the perception of implicit government backing arises from a fairly standard set of attributes for all GSEs, any one GSE may be part of a larger system that the government considers too big to fail. In other words the government is likely to rescue even a smaller GSE before it defaults in its obligations for fear that investors would otherwise lose confidence in the entire agency credit market and the value of the whole $2 trillion in GSE securities might come crashing down. The government's rescue of the failed Farm Credit System in the mid-1980s and the bailout of the smallest institution with GSE attributes, the Financing Corporation, or FICO, in 1996 reinforced investor perception that the government indeed stood behind obligations with a perceived implicit government guarantee.

Consequences for GSEs of the
Implicit Government Guarantee

The implicit federal guarantee is an ingenious device. It permits the government to convey a substantial subsidy to GSEs but that subsidy fails to appear in the federal budget. By providing its guarantee without charge to the GSEs, the government lends the immense power of its creditworthiness to these private companies. According to Congressional Budget Office estimates, the implicit government guarantee conveyed a benefit of $13.6 billion to Fannie Mae, Freddie Mac, and the Federal Home Loan Banks in 2000 alone.[9] As the GSEs increase the amount of their debt securities and MBSs outstanding, the value of the implicit guarantee increases as well.

The government's implicit backing permits GSEs to borrow at much less cost than other companies. GSEs borrow at spreads of perhaps a quarter of a percentage point more than Treasury obligations, which carry the full faith and credit of the federal government. The slight spread over Treasuries results from the implicit nature of the government's backing and from investors' perceptions that an option exists, in theory at least, that the government might refuse to bail out investors in the obligations of a failed GSE. In the terms familiar from the market for state and local obligations, *Treasuries* are a general obligation of the federal government; by contrast *GSE obligations* are what might be called a moral obligation of the government.

The spread in pricing of GSE obligations over Treasuries also relates to the liquidity of the obligations. To the extent that a wide market exists for GSE obligations, investors are willing to receive lower yields in return for the ability to buy and sell the obligations easily and find willing sellers or purchasers. The largest GSEs are taking advantage of recent federal surpluses and the reduction in outstanding Treasury obligations. Fannie Mae and Freddie Mac are issuing large volumes of so-called benchmark obligations in maturities that investors tend to prefer. To the extent that the benchmark obligations begin to rival Treasuries in outstanding volume and liquidity, the GSEs can reduce their borrowing costs by tightening spreads over Treasuries.[10]

The perception of government backing permits the GSEs to operate with much higher leverage than other companies: investors in GSE obligations look to the government's guarantee rather than to the financial strength of a GSE as the basis for repayment. Unless the government sets capital standards to constrain leverage, especially the investor-owned GSEs will have an incentive to keep their leverage higher than investors would otherwise consider prudent without a perception of government backing. The government's implicit guarantee substitutes for equity capital that investors would otherwise require a private company to hold. Essentially

the government serves as a silent equity partner to GSE shareholders by providing financial backing that, according to Congressional
Budget Office calculations, is equivalent to a government contribution of tens of billions of dollars of equity capital—for which the
government requires no financial return.[11]

The government's implicit backing can encourage GSE risk taking in other ways besides high leverage. Normally the market imposes discipline on companies and dampens their ability to take
financial risks. If investors in a company's obligations perceive that
the company has adopted risky financial strategies, they will require
higher returns before they lend money to the company and purchase its obligations. At some point investors may determine that a
company is so risky that they will not purchase its obligations at
any price.

The federal government's guarantee dampens market discipline. Shareholders of a GSE can increase their returns by increasing risks and can leverage these returns by greatly increasing the
ratio of outstanding debt to shareholder equity. Even if risky funding strategies turn into losses as happened to Fannie Mae in the
early 1980s and the Farm Credit System in the mid-1980s, a GSE
can continue to borrow money and issue debt obligations and MBSs
at favorable rates. The federal government receives no compensation when GSEs take increased risks but bears potentially unlim-
ited liability if a GSE fails.

Since 1980 three significant examples of major financial problems at a GSE have occurred: the financial losses suffered by Fannie
Mae in the early 1980s, the inability of the FCS to meet its financial
obligations in the mid-1980s, and the collapse of Freddie Mac's
multifamily loan program in 1989–1990. In two of the cases, external factors precipitated financial difficulties. Much as the thrift industry did, Fannie Mae suffered after the Federal Reserve Board
dramatically increased interest rates in 1979. The FCS took substantial losses because of a deep agricultural recession in the early
1980s. In both cases imprudent financial practices exacerbated the
impact of the external shocks. Fannie Mae was vulnerable to an
interest rate shock because it was holding a large portfolio of long-
term mortgages that it was funding with much shorter-term obligations. Freddie Mac by contrast weathered the increase in interest
rates thanks to its policy of funding mortgages through mortgage-
backed securities rather than a large portfolio. The Farm Credit
System exhibited a range of poor practices including poor man-

agement of credit risk and a policy that led the FCS to fund mortgages at rates substantially below the rates charged by competing commercial banks.[12]

The failure of the Freddie Mac multifamily loan program resulted directly from poor management practices. Freddie Mac applied techniques from its single-family mortgage business to the quite different business of funding income-producing properties. When the dust settled, Freddie Mac had taken a loss of $278 million on its multifamily program. The GSE closed down the program, terminated the staff, and took some years to start over in purchasing multifamily mortgages. Fortunately the multifamily program was only 3 percent of the GSE's business at the time, and the loss could be contained even though it swept the entire program.[13]

Some important lessons emerge from the failures. First, a financial institution may, and often does, appear highly profitable before financial vulnerability becomes apparent. The federal bank and thrift regulators consider high growth rates an important indicator of possible financial risks at an institution. High rates of growth characterized the GSEs in all three cases. Second, the GSEs are confined by their charters to dealing in limited types of financial products. Fannie Mae and Freddie Mac deal in home mortgage loans, the FCS deals in agricultural loans, and so forth. Such financial specialization removes a form of diversification that can help an institution absorb financial shocks. To take the most prominent recent example, the financially specialized thrift industry—not the more diversified commercial banks—collapsed after the Federal Reserve Board raised interest rates in 1979. (Other factors contributed to the divergent outcome: thrifts made fixed rate loans while many commercial bank loans were at variable rates that reset after interest rates rose. But the thrifts' lack of financial diversity remains a major contributor to the early stages of the debacle.) When Freddie Mac made systematic management errors, they replicated themselves across the GSE's entire portfolio of multifamily loans.

Third, the elapsed time between the first signs of problems and heavy losses may be short. Once a GSE has made a systematic mistake and the first signs of loss appear, the rest of the problems will likely manifest themselves soon thereafter. The reports of the Farm Credit Administration on the financial state of the FCS turn from rosy optimism in 1982 to a report of financial stress in 1984 and a request for taxpayer help in 1985.[14] The problems of the Freddie Mac multifamily program and Fannie Mae similarly materialized quickly.

Finally, for GSEs as for other firms, feedback is a gift. Warning signs were present before Fannie Mae faltered and before the FCS failed in the 1980s. Yet the responsible GSE regulators lacked the mandate to act, and the GSEs continued to build their growing businesses on unsound practices.[15]

The perception of the government's implicit backing can keep a GSE in business even after it fails. Spreads over Treasuries did widen somewhat in the financially troubled period before the Farm Credit System declared in 1985 that it could not meet its obligations. Yet the borrowing costs of the FCS remained below yields on A-rated corporate bonds. After the FCS recorded losses of $4.6 billion for 1985 and 1986, Farm Credit System securities remained eligible investments for AAA-rated debt.[16] Similarly, in 1981 Fannie Mae recorded a positive stock value of $500 million, even though the company had a market value net worth that was negative $10.8 billion. The Department of Housing and Urban Development reported that on a market value basis Fannie Mae had a negative net worth for seven consecutive years.[17] The implicit government guarantee may be attractive as a device for conferring a subsidy; conversely the device entails financial risks that the government may not be able to handle before an institution gets into financial trouble.

Managing the Government's Implicit Guarantee

In its financial effects, particularly the way that it dampens market discipline, the government's implicit guarantee of GSE obligations is comparable to federal deposit insurance for banks and thrift institutions. As with federal deposit insurance, the government must attempt to compensate for the loss of market discipline by setting capital standards and supervising the risks taken by GSEs. Otherwise, as in the legislated rescue of the Farm Credit System, the political process is likely to find itself called on to commit taxpayer resources to make good on the obligations of a failing GSE.

The government's efforts to manage the implicit guarantee of GSE obligations both resemble deposit insurance and differ from it. One resemblance relates to the government's need to address the problem of regulatory arbitrage. The relative flexibility of the private sector vis-à-vis the public sector, except in unusual times, permits private companies to engineer their financial activities to deal with virtually any government regulatory requirement.

The federal bank regulators have found that specific legal requirements are especially difficult to maintain in today's fluid financial markets. Private institutions simply devise new financial approaches to arbitrage against fixed requirements, such as the risk-based capital standards that the bank regulators promulgated pursuant to the Basle Accords,[18] and avoid their impact. Similarly Fannie Mae and Freddie Mac are likely to use financial transactions to minimize the impact of the rigid statutory standard for risk-based capital that the Office for Federal Housing Enterprise Oversight (OFHEO) is attempting to apply.

One response, albeit incomplete, to the problem of regulatory arbitrage is to confer discretion on federal regulators to apply flexible remedies in unforeseen circumstances. Federal financial supervision of banks and thrift institutions includes five major components: (1) financial disclosure and reporting requirements; (2) examination of financial condition and risk taking; (3) effective capital requirements, including the authority to require an institution to set aside additional capital to address unusual financial risk; (4) enforcement powers, including the authority to disapprove high-risk activities; and (5) the authority to reorganize or close a troubled institution. In all those areas the federal bank regulators have considerable discretion whether or how to carry out their statutory authority.[19]

An important basis for the success of federal supervision is the mindset of the regulated institutions. In the aftermath of the mistakes of the Farm Credit System, Congress enacted legislation to give the Farm Credit Administration a mandate and powers similar to those of federal bank regulators. Many of today's leaders of the Farm Credit System were impressed by that experience and have not forgotten the lessons. By contrast most other GSEs and their senior managers seem to find government oversight of their businesses nothing but an unwanted intrusion. In the battle over legislation to create the OFHEO, for example, Fannie Mae and Freddie Mac expended considerable effort to limit the discretion of the regulator.[20]

The original Treasury version of the Housing Enterprises Federal Financial Safety and Soundness Act,[21] as well as the version drafted by the General Accounting Office,[22] provided that the regulator would have discretion, comparable to that of federal bank regulators, to examine the GSEs, to impose capital requirements commensurate with the risk that they found, and to enforce the law regarding unsafe and unsound conditions. In contrast to the proposed legislation and in contrast to the laws administered by federal bank regulators, the final legislation that established OFHEO gravely limits the government's discretion. The law also limits OFHEO's capacity by subjecting the agency to the federal appropriations process, in which the GSEs may participate from time to time as a means of bringing pressure on the regulator.[23]

The law also limits the government's ability to set capital standards for Fannie Mae and Freddie Mac. Federal bank regulators are authorized to exercise discretion to adjust the capital requirements that they apply to any particular bank according to the regulator's assessment of the amount of risk in the regulated institution and its activities. By contrast OFHEO must apply a tightly constrained capital standard tied to limited specifications of credit risk and interest rate risk that generate much lower capital requirements than are realistic.

Federal bank regulators have access to a panoply of enforcement powers that they may apply to deal with unsafe and unsound practices and conditions at a regulated institution.[24] By contrast OFHEO's exercise of enforcement powers, except in emergency, is based primarily on the capital levels of the GSEs. The constraint greatly limits the government's authority to deal with problems in advance. Capital levels are a lagging indicator of safety and soundness. The problem is compounded by the provision of OFHEO's authorizing law that deems the GSEs to be adequately capitalized and thus not subject to most of the enforcement provisions until such time as OFHEO can issue a final capital regulation for Fannie Mae and Freddie Mac.

Federal bank regulators also have the authority to place a failed financial institution into conservatorship or receivership, depending on the regulator's judgment of the extent of recovery. By contrast OFHEO has the authority to place a failed GSE into conservatorship but no explicit authority to wind up its operations. The ultimate sanction of dissolution, which applies to virtually all other private companies that fail, does not apply by statute to Fannie Mae or Freddie Mac.

In 1999 Congress enacted legislation that contributes to a similarly flawed supervisory system for the safety and soundness of the Federal Home Loan Banks. The law confers on the Federal Housing Finance Board statutory powers that, with some variations, are generally much more limited than those available to federal bank regulators. Given the lack of experience of the Federal Home Loan Banks at underwriting credit, the combination of weak federal oversight, inadequate capital standards, and expanded financial powers does not bode well for the continued success of the Federal Home Loan Bank System.

The government's implicit guarantee would be difficult to manage even if OFHEO and the other GSE regulators had the mandate, capacity, and authority available to federal bank regulators. A government regulator faces many hurdles in gaining access to the most relevant information about the safety and soundness of a financial institution. The problem of so-called information asymmetries between a financial institution and its regulator is substantial.[25]

To some extent, bank regulators attempt to address the problem by applying lessons from the failure of a single institution to the analysis of the others that they supervise. A bank regulator that may oversee thousands of institutions can gain some information by combining similar institutions into peer groups and then comparing them. By contrast, with only two institutions to supervise—both of which are too big to fail—OFHEO lacks much of the bank regulators' ability to learn from the experiences of a number of institutions or to test financial ratios of Fannie Mae or Freddie Mac against a comparable peer group. It is an open question whether new technologies are widening or helping to reduce the gap in knowledge of financial condition between an institution's managers and its regulator. For a GSE regulator such as OFHEO, with its limited access to appropriate technologies, systems, and information, the gap seems to be widening.

The Institutional Structure for Overseeing Safety and Soundness

The oversight of GSEs is dispersed among a number of federal organizations:

- *Department of the Treasury.* At least in theory, Treasury approves the issuance of GSE obligations (except for the Farm Credit System, which issues obligations on approval of the Farm Credit Administration). Treasury also oversees the safety and soundness of Sallie Mae.
- *Department of Housing and Urban Development.* HUD has general regulatory authority over Fannie Mae and Freddie Mac to ensure that the purposes of their charter acts are carried out and regulates their achievement of affordable housing goals.
- *Farm Credit Administration.* The FCA regulates safety and soundness of the institutions of the Farm Credit System and of Farmer Mac and has general regulatory authority to ensure that the purposes of their charter acts are carried out.
- *Federal Housing Finance Board.* The board regulates safety and soundness of the institutions of the Federal Home Loan Bank

System and has general regulatory authority to ensure that the purposes of their charter acts are carried out. The board oversees an affordable housing fund supported by a 10 percent tax on annual income of the Federal Home Loan Banks.

• *Office of Federal Housing Enterprise Oversight.* OFHEO supervises the safety and soundness of Fannie Mae and Freddie Mac and enforces compliance with their charter acts.

The regulatory structure makes sense only in the context of congressional politics and organization. Over the years the major authorizing committees have established GSEs within their jurisdictions: the agriculture committees created the FCS and Farmer Mac, the banking committees authorized the Federal Home Loan Banks, the housing subcommittees of the banking committees established Fannie Mae and Freddie Mac, and the education and labor committees authorized Sallie Mae. Other committees have been less successful: the small business committees attempted to establish a new GSE and saw the legislation fail when fundamental flaws became apparent.[26]

On the one hand, holding regulators accountable to congressional committees that concern themselves with housing or agriculture or education can help to increase the sensitivity of a regulator to the special needs of those sectors. On the other hand, spreading the regulation of GSEs among many small government offices and agencies is not helpful in protecting the government and taxpayers from unnecessary financial exposure. As Treasury pointed out in a 1991 study of GSEs:

> The problem of avoiding capture appears to be particularly acute in the case of regulation of GSEs. The principal GSEs are few in number; they have highly qualified staffs; they have strong support for their programs from special interest groups; and they have significant resources with which to influence political outcomes. A weak financial regulator would find GSE political power overwhelming and even the most powerful and respected government agencies would find regulating such entities a challenge.[27]

To address the need for the regulator to have the capacity and the mandate to act, both Treasury and the General Accounting Office have recommended that one single regulator oversee the safety and soundness of the six GSEs and their provision of financial services to these sectors. Treasury Undersecretary Robert Glauber recommended in 1991 that the regulation of GSEs be placed in the Treasury Department, the Federal Deposit Insurance Corporation, or the Board of Governors of the Federal Reserve System, institutions that he considered would have the strength to carry out an important but not necessarily popular mission. Of the three, Treasury is likely the most appropriate regulator: it has significant capacity without possessing another major mission such as implementation of monetary policy that could conflict with oversight of safety and soundness of the GSEs.

GAO also proposed centralizing the oversight of all six GSEs but suggested that Congress create an independent agency with the prominence and powers of the Federal Deposit Insurance Corporation.[28] It may be appropriate to add to that recommendation and establish a GSE deposit insurance corporation, comparable to the FDIC insurance funds for banks and thrift institutions. The GSEs would be assessed annual premiums, ideally including risk-adjusted premiums as well as assessments based on size. The premiums would help to fund a reserve fund to provide a cushion in the event that a GSE were to fail and require an infusion of money to pay off outstanding obligations. The joint fund would help to diversify financial risk across all GSEs, at least somewhat, and would create an incentive for each GSE to pay attention to the financial risks being incurred by the other GSEs. To protect the fund from a possible takeover by the government and also to reduce the chance that the fund could contribute to the perception of government backing, money in the fund should be privately owned, even though based on mandatory contributions. The government has already created a modest version of such an insurance corporation in the establishment of the Farm Credit System Insurance Corporation, again as a part of the 1987 legislation to restructure the FCS on a more sound financial footing.[29]

While the centralized financial regulation of all GSEs would be an important way to help protect financial safety and soundness, the change would require congressional leaders to obtain the concurrence, or at least the acquiescence, of the interested authorizing committees. In the early 1990s, in the legislative struggle to create OFHEO, the housing subcommittees were especially vociferous in their efforts to defeat the creation of a central financial regulator. Their willingness to create OFHEO at all can be seen as a defensive measure to forestall a credible threat that the House Ways and Means

Committee would improve oversight of safety and soundness of the GSEs if they did not.[30]

The powerful and technically capable Ways and Means Committee worked with the congressional budget committees and the Senate Banking Committee to induce the authorizing committees to improve financial oversight of the GSEs.[31] The Ways and Means Committee also obtained the enactment of a piece of reform legislation for future GSEs, attached to a larger bill that the president vetoed.[32] The committee differs from the congressional authorizing committees such as agriculture, banking, and education and labor: Ways and Means has not tried to create its own GSE. As the committee of Congress that must raise revenues to pay for a financial bailout, it believed that it had a direct stake in ensuring that the government properly oversaw GSE safety and soundness.

Special Problems of Implicit Government Backing

The implicit government guarantee of GSE obligations is a peculiar device, one that is difficult for the government to manage. First, the implicit guarantee involves careful subtleties that may be hard for people to grasp if they are not specialists in the arcane details of the GSE as an instrument of federal policy.[33] Second, the implicit nature of the implied federal guarantee complicates policymakers' efforts to address the issue of GSE safety and soundness in an explicit manner. Harold Seidman observes: "While called 'private,' these enterprises really function in a *terra incognita*, somewhere between the public and private sectors.... These maverick organizations are able to exploit the ambiguity of their legal status to eliminate or reduce accountability to the government, their shareholders . . . and the public."[34]

Third, the political process does not handle probabilities well. Members of Congress may be insensitive to the results of the regulator's actions in reducing the chances of financial difficulties; by contrast they are likely to be instantly sensitive to any actions of the regulator that reduce immediate benefits to constituents. Financial services legislation generally encounters that problem. Much of the major financial legislation of the United States has related to actual events rather than the anticipation and avoidance of a financial crisis.[35]

The regulator's task is not always popular. To be effective, a regulator may need to intervene and limit excessive risk-taking by a company that appears to be running well.[36] The financial difficulties of several financial institutions, including thrifts during the thrift debacle and Fannie Mae in the late 1970s, illustrate that a period of apparently high profits can mask the emergence of conditions that will cause financial distress. Without a mandate to act preventatively, a government regulator will find it hard to deal with such situations.

One consequence of the emphasis on the present benefit of GSEs over their potential costs is a reluctance of the authorizing committees to require GSEs to increase capital significantly above levels that the GSEs would adopt on their own. The authorizing committees are well aware that "their" GSEs compete in a world of what Freddie Mac's Robert Van Order calls "dueling charters." Low capital standards are an easy way to increase the value of the unbudgeted government subsidy to the GSEs and their constituencies at a cost of potential risks that may not materialize while the relevant officials are still in office. Of all GSEs, only the Farm Credit System appears to be subject to capital standards close to the level that the government now applies to other financial services firms in a similar line of business. The ability of the Farm Credit Administration to apply such standards today would seem to relate to the financial failure of the FCS in the 1980s and to the strong hand that Treasury took in crafting the remedial legislation in 1987.

Another consequence is the difficulty for a financial regulator such as OFHEO to be certain that, should a GSE get into financial trouble, the relevant policymakers would support rather than impede efforts to resolve the crisis in any way that disadvantaged the GSE's shareholders.[37] The political power of the GSEs and their resentment of government second-guessing of their business strategies make the problem special. As seen from GSE attacks on government agencies and offices such as Treasury and the CBO,[38] a financial regulator for the GSEs requires a strong mandate, backed by political support, to be successful in carrying out its responsibilities.

Prudent reforms of GSE financial supervision have unfortunately proved difficult for policymakers to enact. The government continues to create the preconditions for a state of risk. The GSEs and their unusual form of government subsidy provide a case study of the inability of the political process to take modest steps now to improve the government's ability to deal with the slight but real probability that a GSE could fail at a substantial cost.

The government's implicit guarantee also affects the ability of policymakers to improve the public benefits that GSEs provide. HUD, for example, has been reluctant to impose serious affordable housing requirements on Fannie Mae and Freddie Mac. As the GAO reported, "A HUD official said that the Department's conservative approach was necessary to maintain the enterprises' financial soundness and to ensure that the goals could be met in good economic times as well as bad."[39]

The government can find itself caught in a double bind with the GSEs arguing on financial grounds against serving high-priority public purposes but also arguing against effective financial regulation on the grounds of the potential impact on their ability to serve public purposes if, for example, capital standards were raised.[40] Once the government is perceived as on the hook to pay for financial losses of a company, the government finds it hard to do anything but agree to support the profitability of that company, regardless of the effects on public purposes.

4

The Public Purposes
of GSEs

GSEs differ in their charters from ordinary private companies. An ordinary private company is chartered under the general business corporation laws of a state. Incorporators file articles of incorporation with a state and thereby consent to the state's jurisdiction in legal matters. Normally articles of incorporation are general in scope so that an incorporated company can freely adjust its business activities to market conditions without the formality of filing an amendment.

By contrast GSEs operate under unique federal laws and charters. The theory of GSEs seems to be that their government subsidies should help them to serve public purposes defined by law. The laws provide them with special benefits, and in return each GSE accepts the limitations of a special-purpose charter that is comparable in legal structure to the authorizing laws that prescribe the permitted activities of a federal agency. In contrast to the ordinary private company, the GSE is authorized to exercise only those powers prescribed in its enabling legislation.[1]

GSE charter acts create a fairly rigid structure compared with state corporation laws. Consider first the express powers of GSEs, then the incidental powers, and then the legal consequences of acts that go beyond those that are authorized by a GSE's enabling legislation. Finally, it is important to consider the role of the regulator in approving GSE activities, and some of the problems that Congress faces when it attempts to amend GSE charter acts.

Express Powers. GSE charter acts specify the types of activities in which they may engage. Fannie Mae's charter act authorizes it to "purchase, service, sell, lend on the security of, or otherwise deal in" conventional mortgages.[2] A conventional mortgage is not insured or guaranteed by a federal government agency such as the Federal Housing Administration or Department of Veterans Affairs; the authority to deal in such government mortgages is contained in another part of the charter act.

The concept of the secondary mortgage market is essentially a legal one rather than a product of the free market. In the free market, portfolio lenders may hold the mortgages that they originate or from time to time may sell pools of mortgages to other lenders. By contrast, under their charter acts, Fannie Mae and Freddie Mac are supposed to be secondary market institutions, that is, companies that deal with lenders that originate mortgages but do not deal directly with the borrowers or make mortgage loans directly to them. Fannie Mae and Freddie Mac may purchase mortgages but may not originate mortgages.

As in all authorizing legislation, Congress can sometimes be quite specific in setting limitations on authorized powers. Fannie Mae and Freddie Mac may not deal in single-family mortgages larger than a statutory mortgage limit in their charter acts. The statutory limit takes the form of a formula that reflects the average prices of new homes in the United States, as determined by a federal regulator, the Office of Federal Housing Enterprise Oversight. For the year 2002 the so-called conforming mortgage limit for a single-family home is $300,700.

The Fannie Mae and Freddie Mac charter acts also specify that the two GSEs may fund only mortgages meeting the purchase standards of private institutional investors and that the mortgages must be for residential property of specified types.

Finally, the Fannie Mae and Freddie Mac charter acts authorize the two firms to hold mortgages in portfolio and either fund them with agency-status debt or sell them in pools of mortgage-backed securities. The charter acts do not say "agency status" in so many words. Instead they provide for the various attributes, such as the SEC exemption and issuance on approval of the Treasury Department, that help to constitute agency status (see table 3-1). Provisions of other laws, such as amendments to the National Bank Act that permit national banks to purchase GSE obligations without limitation, also contribute to the perception of government backing for GSE obligations and mortgage-backed securities.

The express provisions of the charter acts also impose limitations on their funding activities. In contrast to Ginnie Mae, a wholly owned federal government corporation, neither Fannie Mae nor Freddie Mac may guarantee mortgage-backed securities issued by others. Instead Fannie Mae and Freddie Mac must first purchase the mortgages and then sell them as pools that back their guaranteed MBSs.

Some GSEs have greater latitude under their charter acts than others. In contrast to Fannie Mae and Freddie Mac, the Federal Home Loan Banks are not expressly permitted to guarantee mortgage-backed securities or to hold mortgages in their portfolios. In part the limited nature of activities authorized by the Federal Home Loan Bank Act reflects the interests of the financial institutions that own and control the individual Federal Home Loan Banks. Conversely, also in contrast to Fannie Mae and Freddie Mac, the law does not limit the size of mortgage that they may fund.

The major authorized activity of the Federal Home Loan Banks is to provide so-called advances to their member-institutions. An *advance* is a loan from a federal home loan bank to one of its cooperative owner-members. A member-institution, generally a commercial bank or thrift institution, originates mortgages to its customers. The institution then uses the mortgages as collateral to obtain a loan from a federal home loan bank for funds to make yet more mortgage loans.

The advance is a financial product offering limited financial advantage, especially vis-à-vis the ability of Fannie Mae and Freddie Mac to purchase and hold or securitize mortgages. Alex Pollock, president and CEO of the Federal Home Loan Bank of Chicago, reviewed the financial opportunities available to his institution and decided to create a new financial product for his members, the so-called Mortgage Partnership Finance (MPF) program.

Under MPF a member-institution originates a mortgage for the Federal Home Loan Bank of Chicago, provides some credit enhancement, and services the mortgage. The bank uses its access to the agency credit market to issue low-cost debt to fund the mortgage, which appears on the books of the federal home loan bank for its duration. The product enables the bank to compete directly with Fannie Mae and Freddie Mac in purchasing pools of conforming mortgages and has proved especially attractive as a source of funding for FHA loans in place of Ginnie Mae.

The rigidities of GSE authorizing legislation can prompt different responses. Sometimes a GSE simply obtains its own legal opinion and then asserts the right to engage in types of activity unforeseen when the legislation originally was enacted. As discussed later, a regulator, such as the Federal Housing Finance Board, the regulator of the Federal Home Loan Banks, may issue regulations or opinions to try to expand a GSE's permitted activities. Under the case law a court may often give greater deference to the determination of a federal regulator than to a GSE's unilateral decision.

Incidental Powers. GSEs are merely one form of instrumentality that operates under special charter legislation. Other instrumentalities operate under similar authorizing laws. The perennial congressional debates about the powers of commercial banks reflect the fact that banks too—and thrift institutions and credit unions—may exercise only those powers that are authorized by law.[3] As reflected in the case law, judicial interpretations relating to the scope of incidental bank powers may have relevance to interpretations of the implied powers of GSEs.

The issue of incidental or implied powers arises because as in any authorizing legislation, Congress cannot consider every contingency that the legislation must address for GSEs or other financial institutions. In addition to the express powers of each GSE spelled out in law, the enabling legislation authorizes the GSE to exercise powers incidental to the express powers. The Fannie Mae charter act authorizes the company "to do all things as are necessary or incidental to the proper management of its affairs and the proper conduct of its business."[4]

Sallie Mae has a more sweeping legislative grant of authority than the other GSEs or for other federally chartered financial institutions.[5] The Sallie Mae charter act authorizes it "to undertake any . . . activity the Board of Directors of the Association determines to be in furtherance of the programs of . . . student loans . . . authorized under this part or will otherwise support the credit needs of students."[6]

Relatively few court cases interpret the scope of incidental powers of GSEs. In several cases the courts have held that plaintiffs lacked the requisite standing to challenge acts of a GSE that they considered to be beyond the scope of their enabling legislation.[7] When the federal regulator has approved an activity, as with the MPF program of the Federal Home Loan Bank of Chicago, standing is then easier to achieve, on the grounds that the regulator may have violated the Administrative Procedure Act in approving the challenged activity.[8] If a GSE charter act prohibits certain activities, representatives of the industry that performs such activities in competition with the GSE may have standing to challenge the activities as beyond the scope of the GSE's authority.[9]

The few cases that do decide questions of the incidental powers of GSEs tend to rely on the precedents in cases involving other instrumentalities, especially national banks. The leading case, involving national banks, remains *Arnold Tours v. Camp*.[10] The court held that an activity of a national bank was properly incidental to an express power if it was "convenient or useful" in carrying out that power.[11]

If a GSE such as Fannie Mae seeks to develop an automated mortgage underwriting system, a court is likely to decide that such an activity is convenient or useful in carrying out its express power to purchase mortgages. By contrast a court could have more difficulty finding that an activity such as real estate brokerage, which traditionally has been completely separate from the mortgage lending business, would be properly convenient or useful to carrying out an express charter power.

The origins of the Fannie Mae charter act date to the National Housing Act of 1934, which has since been amended in major ways. In 1954 Fannie Mae became a so-called mixed-ownership corporation of the federal government, and in 1968 Fannie Mae was rechartered as a completely privately owned company.[12] In 1992 Congress again made significant changes to the Fannie Mae charter act as a part of the legislation that created a new financial regulator, the Office of Federal Housing Enterprise Oversight.

The process of legislating and elaborating on earlier legislation has left Fannie Mae with a charter act filled with complicated and detailed provisions. The Freddie Mac charter act, which dates to the Emergency Home Finance Act of 1970, also contains elaborate provisions.[13] Congress frequently amends GSE charter acts to try to deal with unanticipated issues.

As a result of the patchwork of provisions, especially in the older GSE enabling acts, a skilled lawyer can find a justification for many activities not actually contemplated by Congress. Over time, as Congress amends GSE charter acts without objecting to a particular activity, the activity becomes less and less susceptible to successful challenge. New technologies, which change the strategic importance of older activities, unsurprisingly have provided an excellent opportunity for GSEs to engage in what their commercial competitors term mission creep. Backed by immense market power, GSEs can build incidental powers onto express powers and then pyramid other incidental powers, convenient or useful to carrying out the new powers, onto those.

Fannie Mae and Freddie Mac can roll out automated underwriting systems and then, through activities that are convenient or useful to automated underwriting and information-based lending, can displace many activities of the mortgage insurance, appraisal, and title insurance industries. The GSEs greatly expand their roles vis-à-vis the primary mortgage market potentially without running afoul of charter limitations, as illustrated in table 1-1.

Legal Consequences of Unauthorized Acts. On a purely technical basis, a GSE has no authority to engage in acts beyond the scope of its authorized powers, both express and incidental powers. Acts beyond the scope of permitted authority are called *ultra vires*, a term that dates to the midnineteenth century and British cases concerning special purpose charters granted by the British Parliament to railroad companies.

Courts have held that *ultra vires* acts may be void and unenforceable under law. Although many such cases are old,[14] one recent case applied the doctrine to an institution of the Farm Credit System that had entered into a contract beyond the scope of its legal authority.[15] The court held that "because an *ultra vires* contract is null and void, the remedy for rescission of that contract is to put the parties in the position they would have occupied had the unlawful agreement not been made."[16]

In practice a GSE may be able to turn to its government regulator to help resolve issues of uncertainty in a charter act. Early in Fannie Mae's experience as a GSE, the Department of Housing and Urban Development issued regulations to help define matters of shareholder rights that the charter act had failed to address.[17]

More recently the Federal Housing Finance Board approved the Mortgage Partnership Finance Program as properly "incidental" to the authority of a Federal Home Loan Bank to make advances. That position is astonishing, considering that the MPF program will substitute for an advance rather than complement an advance in some incidental way. A court has just upheld the Finance Board action and stated that the Finance Board should define the contours of the term *incidental* when reviewing whether an action of the Federal Home Loan Banks is authorized as an incidental power within the Federal Home Loan Bank Act.[18] The case seems to stand for the proposition that GSE charter acts are so complex that even federal judges may lose their way among the arcane issues that mean so much when a GSE enters new activities.

Under the leading case of *Chevron U.S.A., Inc. v. Natural Resources Defense Council*,[19] courts will give deference to an agency's interpretive regulations in cases where congressional intent is silent or ambiguous.[20] Given the many gaps and unclear provisions of GSE charter acts, courts will likely have considerable opportunity to defer to the appropriate federal agency in cases where the agency has issued an interpretation.[21] The Farm Credit Administration and Federal Housing Finance Board have especially broad latitude to issue regulations to define the authorized powers of the institutions that they supervise.

For a GSE the judicial deference to agency interpretation may be a two-edged sword. On the one hand an enthusiastic regulator such as the Federal Housing Finance Board may be able to issue regulations that help to expand the scope of permitted activities by a GSE under their jurisdiction.[22] On the other hand directors and officers of a GSE are likely to be chilled if a federal regulator decides one day to send each a ruling that asserts that a specific GSE activity is *ultra vires* and thus null and void under the agency's interpretation of the charter act.

Agency Authority to Approve New Programs and Activities of a GSE. Most GSE charter acts permit a designated federal agency to approve new programs or activities. The notable exception is Sallie Mae; its charter act expressly denies authority to the relevant federal government departments to approve its activities: "Nothing in this section shall be construed so as to authorize the Secretary of Education or the Secretary of the Treasury to limit, control, or constrain programs of the Association or support of the Guaranteed Student Loan Program by the Association."[23]

For the other GSEs, approval provisions come in two general forms: (1) express authority to approve new activities and (2) general regulatory authority to see that the purposes of a GSE charter act are carried out. Fannie Mae and Freddie Mac are subject to both types of provision.

For new product approval, the 1992 Federal Housing Enterprises Financial Safety and Soundness Act provides that "the Secretary [of Housing and Urban Development] shall require each enterprise to obtain the approval of the Secretary for any new program of the enterprise before implementing the program"[24] Regarding general regulatory authority, that act provides

> Except for the authority of the Director of the Office of Federal Housing Enterprise Oversight . . . and all other matters relating to the safety and soundness of the enterprises, the Secretary of Housing and Urban Development shall have general regulatory power over each enterprise and shall make such rules and regulations as shall be necessary and proper to assure that this part and the purposes of the Federal National Mortgage Association Charter Act and the Federal Home Loan Mortgage Corporation Charter Act are accomplished.[25]

In concept those provisions confer substantial authority on the secretary of housing and urban development to direct the activities of Fannie Mae and Freddie Mac to serve high-priority public purposes. The courts have conferred on federal agencies considerable authority to use their discretion in applying general regulatory authority.[26] The advent of new technology should give the department frequent opportunity to approve or disapprove new programs that reflect the new ways that GSEs and other financial institutions seek to provide financial services.

When it chartered Fannie Mae as a GSE in 1968, Congress intended that HUD use its regulatory leverage to direct the company's activities to serve high-priority public purposes, and HUD continues to have this responsibility. In 1976 HUD Secretary Carla Hills sent a memorandum to Senator William Proxmire, chairman of the Senate Banking Committee, that nicely summarized HUD's statutory responsibilities regarding oversight of the activities and operations of Fannie Mae at that time. She pointed to a number of statutory provisions and the following legislative history:

> During Senate Committee hearings leading to the enactment of the 1968 Housing Act, then HUD Secretary Robert Weaver made the following relevant statements:
>
> "The Secretary would have general regulatory power over the new private corporation."
>
> "He would be able to veto some of the decisions. He would not be able to take the positive or other side of it

and say, 'invest here,' or 'buy that,' but he could say, 'don't borrow now.' He would have control over the borrowing capacity as well as the individual borrowings, and this would be his major leverage over the new corporation." [27]

Legislative amendments have greatly reduced HUD's leverage. In a noncontroversial technical amendment, Congress in 1984 repealed the secretary's authority to approve Fannie Mae's issuance of stock, obligations, and other securities. The Treasury Department does retain statutory authority to approve the issuance of debt obligations by the GSEs and the interest rates and maturities of such obligations.

The decades since 1970 have seen a progression of amendments that have weakened the government's control over Fannie Mae and Freddie Mac. The change in legislative framework both reflects the general political weakness of the Department of Housing and Urban Development vis-à-vis the GSEs and compounds HUD's efforts at oversight. The department for many years did not play any significant role in promoting GSE service to high-priority public purposes. Instead the department stood by and watched in the 1990s as the GSEs used their competitive advantages to expand into areas previously off limits.[28]

Action at the end of the decade may indicate that the department has begun to reconsider its stance. In letters to Fannie Mae and Freddie Mac, HUD requested that the two GSEs submit information about two new programs that they had begun to implement without regard to HUD's authority to approve such programs in advance.[29]

The Role of Technological Convergence. New technologies are changing the nature of financial services fundamentally. Lenders must base their relationships with customers on information-based analysis. The mining of databases permits lenders to assess risk in new and sophisticated ways. Banking industry strategists point out that technologies are forcing a convergence in financial services, such that communications, information, and computing are helping to integrate once distinct financial services.[30] Technological convergence means that financial services begin to overlap among banks, insurance companies, GSEs, and other financial services providers. On the basis of new technologies, firms gain the capacity to offer new products. The developments were already perceptible in the 1970s, when new information systems allowed financial services firms to develop money market mutual funds to compete with banks and thrifts on the liability side of the balance sheet and to use securitization to compete on the asset side.[31] Banks and thrifts have subsequently experienced an increasing squeeze on the profits from serving as financial intermediaries.

New technologies also offer the opportunity for federal instrumentalities to expand the scope of their activities. With imagination, financial services companies and government regulators can fill the venerable language of an authorizing statute with completely new meaning. The Comptroller of the Currency was able to characterize a life insurance annuity contract as a financial investment product rather than insurance. The Supreme Court agreed that the sale of such a product was equivalent to traditional activity in the business of banking and therefore national banks could offer annuity contracts for sale.[32]

Fannie Mae was able to persuade HUD that a program of providing credit life, disability, and involuntary unemployment insurance for borrowers fell within the scope of the Fannie Mae charter act. HUD determined that the provision of such insurance to borrowers whose mortgages Fannie Mae funded would be within the scope of Fannie Mae's statutory authority to "deal in" conventional mortgages.[33]

Freddie Mac has been able to take advantage of the fact that financial institutions today carry out their activities in ways not contemplated in the language of the charter acts. Freddie Mac defends its investment in HomeAdvisor Technologies, a spin-off venture of the Microsoft Corporation, as follows: "HomeAdvisor is not a loan originator, but simply a distribution channel for the technology platform, and all of the loans that come through the platform will still need to be funded and closed by Freddie Mac seller/servicers."[34]

But the Freddie Mac statement leaves something unsaid: Freddie Mac and its Internet partner will provide much of the value-added that the seller-servicer formerly provided as a part of mortgage origination. Primary mortgage lenders and service providers (such as appraisers and providers of other settlement services) are finding themselves squeezed between emerging Internet-based shopping on the one hand and the market power of the GSEs on the other.

The Federal Housing Finance Board has been especially active at reinterpreting the charter act of the Federal Home Loan Bank System. The board's approval of the Mortgage Partnership Finance program was noted earlier. That decision sets a significant precedent, which allows the system banks to fund mortgage loans directly on their own balance sheets, potentially in competition with financial institutions that are members of other Federal Home Loan Banks.

The board also issued regulations to permit its supervised banks to issue or confirm letters of credit, again as a purported substitute for express powers, including the authority to make collateralized advances, which are authorized in the Federal Home Loan Bank Act. Letters of credit can be used to enhance the credit rating of securities and otherwise support securitization, which is an express power that the Federal Home Loan Banks do not have under the Federal Home Loan Bank Act.

The Process of Charter Act Expansion. The GSEs have proved themselves adept at obtaining expansions of their charter act authority. They present proposed changes to Congress as minor technical amendments or as means of enhancing services provided to consumers. In 1974, 1977, and 1980 Fannie Mae obtained technical amendments to expand its charter powers. In contrast to the original limitations, Fannie Mae may now use a larger base amount plus a one-way escalator as the basis for the formula for determining the size limit for the conforming mortgages that it is eligible to purchase.[35] Moreover, the provision links the formula to new home prices rather than the lower average prices for the mix of new and resale homes that the GSE helped to finance. As a result the fraction of the conventional mortgage market that Fannie Mae is permitted to serve (along with Freddie Mac, which obtained the parallel provision in its charter) has dramatically increased.

In 1989, in the aftermath of the savings and loan debacle, Fannie Mae obtained a charter amendment that altered its public purposes from a limiting statement ("provide supplementary assistance to the secondary market for home mortgages") to a bland one ("respond appropriately to the private capital market").[36] Virtually no one opposed the change, even though it provided statutory support for Fannie Mae (and then Freddie Mac, which obtained the same statement of public purpose) to justify the substantial displacement of portfolio lenders in the primary market for conforming mortgages, notably banks and thrift institutions, by the two secondary market GSEs. The change ended an effort by HUD to use the supplementary assistance provision to limit Fannie Mae's activities so that the GSE would not displace activities of private firms in the mortgage market without government sponsorship.[37]

One recent amendment to the charter act illustrates the dangers of legislative enactment of provisions whose consequences only the GSEs understand. The 1999 amendment to the Freddie Mac charter act actually became law, but Congress was forced to reverse the new legislation only two weeks later.

In the closing days of the 105th Congress, Freddie Mac secured enactment of a charter act amendment to allow it to bear the financial risk on low–down-payment mortgages rather than meeting the requirement of private mortgage insurance. Since 1970 the charter acts of both Freddie Mac and Fannie Mae had provided that when they purchased a conventional mortgage, each GSE would need to be sure that private mortgage insurance covered any credit risk above an 80 percent loan-to-value ratio. Freddie Mac's change would permit the GSE to take that credit risk for itself and eliminate any requirement for private mortgage insurance.

Freddie Mac obtained the support of Alfonse D'Amato, the chairman of the Senate Banking Committee, who supervised the addition of the Freddie Mac amendment to a bill in a House-Senate conference at the final stages of its legislative process.[38] President Bill Clinton signed the bill into law shortly thereafter. If it had stood, the Freddie Mac amendment would have permitted Freddie Mac to take over much of the value-added that is the core business of many mortgage insurance companies. Faced with a sudden drop in the value of their companies, the mortgage insurance industry mounted a hasty campaign to reverse the provision.[39]

The examples highlight important lessons about GSE powers today. First, the provisions of GSE legislation are arcane and often poorly understood, even by the legislators who sponsor them and the members of the congressional committees who vote for them.

Second, seemingly slight changes in a GSE charter can have substantial implications for the financial system. Policymakers often do not appreciate how such changes to a GSE charter can cause sweeping changes in the financial markets.

GSEs can make an appealing argument for change, for example, that it would enable the entity to offer more services at lower cost. The argument, based as it is on the ability of the GSE to funnel government subsidies into the new activities, can obscure the larger implications. The GSEs can enhance the expansiveness of any new legislative language by providing floor statements, committee report language, and other interpretations that become a part of the legislative history in ways that policymakers may not have intended.

Once the change has been enacted, GSEs and some regulators can infuse meaning into the arcane provisions and permit the agencies to move into entirely new lines of business.

Third, in today's fast-moving markets, the GSEs have the capacity to gear up quickly to implement any new powers achieved by legislation or otherwise. Fannie Mae and Freddie Mac rolled out their automated underwriting systems in 1995; by the end of 2000 Freddie Mac had already processed 10 million loans through its automated system. In 2000 Freddie Mac processed 60 percent and Fannie Mae, 56 percent of the GSEs' loan purchases through automated systems. Fannie Mae expects to purchase 80 percent of its loans through its automated system by the year 2003. Such rapid deployment can make it hard for policymakers to revisit decisions and try to roll back activities.

The consequences of misunderstanding by policymakers can be particularly serious when statutory provisions involve safety and soundness. While private competitors of the GSEs may scrutinize legislation that affects them, the government, on behalf of taxpayers, primarily has a direct stake in the quality of supervision of the safety and soundness of a GSE.

A recent example is H.R. 1409, the Secondary Mortgage Market Regulatory Improvements Act, introduced April 5, 2001. On its face it would improve the government's statutory basis for addressing GSE safety and soundness. Among other provisions it transfers to the Federal Reserve Board responsibility for supervision of Fannie Mae and Freddie Mac. However, instead of basing the government's authority on well-tested statutes applicable to federal bank regulators, H.R. 1409 builds on the dubious foundations of the existing statutory structure for oversight of Fannie Mae and Freddie Mac.

The continuing reliance on an unsound foundation will create problems that are not apparent to policymakers. The congressional sponsor of H.R. 1409 states—mistakenly—in a press release that "Congressional appropriations approval is not required" to provide funds for the GSE regulator.[40] But the bill would continue to require that assessments of fees by the regulator be placed in a fund in the Treasury. The Constitution states, in Article I, section 9, that "no money shall be drawn from the Treasury, but in consequence of appropriations made by law."

Even if a court should find that the money going into the Treasury fund were private, the regulator would still need an appropriation to get it out. A court would be buttressed in this conclusion because of other parts of the assessments provision. The congressional sponsor, even if succeeding against the odds in getting his bill enacted, would not achieve his intended results. The trap hidden in the provision would likely be sprung only if the affected parties found themselves in crisis or controversy. If the Federal Reserve Board anticipated receiving responsibility under H.R. 1409, its lawyers should take care that the Fed receives a full regulatory toolbox before it tries to carry out its nominal supervisory authority.

Neither Congress nor the executive branch appears to be appropriately equipped to deal with the dangers of legislation that no independent party understands fully and that has the potential to affect the financial markets adversely on a large-scale. The GSEs can create an entirely new dimension of a state of risk. Congress would be well advised to require that the Treasury Department, the General Accounting Office, and the Congressional Budget Office scrutinize and opine on the costs and benefits of GSE legislation, including so-called minor technical amendments, before rather than after the Congress enacts them.

5
Origins of the Legal
Framework of GSEs

Today most corporations organized under state law hold general-purpose charters. The state law of Delaware is typical: it provides that a corporation may engage in virtually any legitimate activity except where restricted or precluded by law.[1] Amid the several million general-purpose corporations active in the United States today are a few thousand special-purpose companies created by or otherwise subject to restrictive state or federal laws. Instrumentalities of government are the surviving vestiges of mercantilist institutions: a government charters them to carry out public purposes specified by law.

Consider first the development of corporate charters in mercantilist times and the early United States and then some lessons that history teaches about the attributes and life cycles of special-purpose institutions compared with ordinary general-purpose companies.

Parts of this chapter are extracted from Thomas H. Stanton, "Nonquantifiable Risks and Financial Institutions: The Mercantilist Legal Framework of Banks, Thrifts, and Government-Sponsored Enterprises," in *Global Risk-Based Capital Regulations*, vol. 1, edited by Charles A. Stone and Anne Zissu (Burr Ridge, Ill.: Irwin Professional Publishing, 1994), pp. 57–97. Reproduced by permission. The author gratefully acknowledges the financial assistance of the Institute for Policy Innovation in preparing an earlier version of this research, published as a monograph, "Taxpayers at Risk: The Moral Hazards of the New Mercantilism" (Lewisville, Tex.: Institute for Policy Innovation, June 1992).

The Mercantilist Origins of
Instrumentalities of Government

In mercantilist Europe, from the sixteenth through the eighteenth centuries, governments had great aspirations but limited institutional capacity. Markets were undeveloped and ineffective in the provision of important products and services. Instead of acting through their own administrative apparatus, governments often chartered companies to carry out many public purposes and activities, including banking, manufacturing, transportation, mining, and trade. Government saw business corporations essentially as agencies of the government.[2]

Merchants with ideas for new ventures would seek an advocate at the royal court to present a plea for a charter. A charter would specify permitted activities and special privileges of the new corporation and would provide that the sovereign would be appropriately compensated for the privileges bestowed. Incorporation generally involved the grant of monopoly powers, including the power to regulate business activities in the company's designated economic sector.

A charter would confer exclusive benefits and include a commitment that the crown would not issue similar charters to competitors. In return for a license of royal privilege, a mercantilist company accepted limits on its permitted activities and committed itself to undertake the particular tasks specified in its royal charter. These were early instrumentalities of government.

As the British Parliament gained in strength, it began to confer more of such charters. Eventually Parliament rather than the monarch decided to bestow corporate charters for new ventures. As before, the charter specified the public purpose of the company, its permitted activities and privileges, and the remuneration to the state. Corporate charters often had a limited life; they might expire at specified events or in a prescribed number of years.

Mercantilist companies included many trading companies such as the East India Company, Hudson's Bay Company, Russia Company, Levant Company, and South Sea Company. Other companies included mining companies, manufacturing companies, and the Bank of England. The early ventures were organized as so-called regulated companies; later ventures developed as joint-stock companies.[3]

Writing in 1776, at the end of the mercantilist period, Adam Smith expressed disapproval of the practice of granting such special charters, especially in regard to commerce:

But in this respect, as in many others, nations have not always acted consistently; and in the greater part of the commercial states of Europe, particular companies of merchants have had the address to persuade the legislature to entrust to them the performance of this part of the duty of the sovereign, together with all of the powers which are necessarily connected with it.

These companies, though they may, perhaps, have been useful for the first introduction of some branches of commerce, by making at their own expense, an experiment which the state might not think it prudent to make, have in the long-run proved, universally, either burdensome or useless, and have either mismanaged or confined the trade.[4]

Since mercantilist times, two important developments have occurred. First, the establishment of centralized administrative states, especially on the continent of Europe, has meant that governments gained the ability to use governmental institutions to carry out public purposes. Both Great Britain and the United States have been somewhat exceptional in their reluctance to build large national bureaucracies. In both countries, governments have continued to rely on instrumentalities to carry out many public functions, especially banking.[5]

Second, starting in the nineteenth century, corporation law in the United States and Great Britain has progressed from particular charters toward the form of general-purpose corporations. While mercantilist companies were permitted to conduct only those activities specified in their charters, general-purpose corporations today may undertake virtually any kind of activity unless precluded by law. While mercantilist charters were granted to a privileged few incorporators, virtually any group of citizens desiring to do so may form a general-purpose corporation today.[6] The latter is a much more flexible system: unlike companies with special and limited charters, general-purpose corporations can adapt their activities and lines of business to meet market needs and do not need to obtain political approval to do so.

Legal Antecedents for Today's GSEs

The earliest corporate charters in the United States followed the European mercantilist model. The Continental Congress chartered the Bank of North America in 1781; because of questions about the authority of the congress to charter a bank, the bank also obtained a charter from the State of Pennsylvania. Within a few years, political opposition to the bank's monopoly powers forced the repeal of its state charter and then limited the terms of a new charter granted by the State of Pennsylvania.[7]

Alexander Hamilton, secretary of the Treasury, proposed the creation of the first Bank of the United States; Congress enacted the legislation in 1791. Hamilton patterned the bank on the Bank of England, chartered in 1694. He justified the bank's existence as an instrument of public policy: "Public utility is more truly the object of public banks than private profit. And it is the business of government to constitute them on such principles that, while the latter will result in a sufficient degree to afford competent motives to engage in them, the former be not made subservient to it."[8]

The charter of the Bank of the United States, limited to a term of twenty years, specified the powers and privileges of the company. The U.S. government was a minority shareholder. When Congress failed to extend the charter, the bank expired in 1811.

State legislatures continued to charter banks. Aaron Burr obtained a perpetual bank charter from the New York State Legislature in 1799: the Manhattan Company was to provide a supply of pure water for the City of New York. Burr used his political skill and influence to obtain a special provision of the charter authorizing the company to use any profits for any purpose not prohibited by the Constitution or laws of the United States or the State of New York. Under this provision Burr established the Manhattan Bank, which later merged into the Chase Manhattan Bank.[9]

In 1816 the federal government enacted legislation to charter a second Bank of the United States, again with the government as a minority shareholder. The twenty-year charter again prescribed the authorized activities of the bank. It also provided that private shareholders would elected the majority of the directors but the president of the United States would appoint five of the twenty directors. The federal charter of the Bank of the United States expired in 1836 after President Andrew Jackson's Bank War, in which he vetoed legislation that would have provided for renewal for another twenty years. As with the first bank war over the Bank of North America, the opposition was fueled by the popular objection to monopoly and privileges bestowed on a favored few shareholders.

The two Banks of the United States are the lineal ancestors of most federal instrumentalities that provide financial services today.

Thus both national banks and government-sponsored enterprises trace their antecedents to these institutions. The Banks of the United States were authorized to serve the entire nation and to make virtually any kinds of loan.[10] Government-sponsored enterprises feature the former characteristic (nationwide scope) and national banks the latter (largely unrestricted kinds of loans). Only in recent years has Congress permitted national banks to expand beyond significant limitations on the geographic areas that individual institutions were permitted to serve.

Indeed the legal case law for both kinds of institution, and for thrifts, other commercial banks, and other federal instrumentalities as well, stems from two great cases involving the second Bank of the United States, *McCulloch v. Maryland* and *Osborn v. Bank of the United States*.[11] Obligations of the first and second Banks of the United States (BUS) were eligible for use in the payment of obligations to the federal government. Some controversy remains about the extent that the market value of United States Bank obligations derived from this feature in its charter act and the extent that market value largely stemmed from the financial soundness of the institution.[12] However, other than that feature, and except for federal investment in BUS stock, implicit federal backing appears to have been absent from BUS obligations.

The second Bank of the United States foreshadowed many of today's government-sponsored enterprises in the structure of the board of directors, consisting of a majority of shareholder-elected directors and a minority of publicly appointed directors. While use of such publicly appointed directors has more logic for government-sponsored enterprises than for the Bank of the United States, the idea remains in disfavor among public administration professionals and others.[13] In contrast to the GSEs today, the charters of both Banks of the United States included a twenty-year sunset provision: operations would terminate unless the charter were extended.

After President Andrew Jackson's war with the Bank of the United States, in which he vetoed the legislation to recharter the second Bank, the federal government left banking issues largely to the states. Only with the advent of the Civil War and the need for money to support the Union struggle did the federal government enact the National Currency Act of 1863 and the National Bank Act of 1864 and thus reenter the field with federally chartered financial institutions.

The national bank system departed from the model of the Bank of the United States and took on a decentralized form. The National

Bank Act provided that any responsible group of incorporators meeting legal requirements could obtain a federal charter without special enabling legislation that had been a feature of the Banks of the United States and that remains a feature of several government-sponsored enterprises.

The national bank system flourished alongside state-chartered banks. Starting with the Panic of 1907, the federal government began exploring institutional reforms. The Federal Reserve Act, signed into law in 1913, created a large but decentralized institution, with many attributes of a government-sponsored enterprise.

Today the Federal Reserve System combines features of a GSE with those of a government agency. On the one hand, similar to the Federal Home Loan Banks, the twelve Federal Reserve Banks are owned and controlled by private users, in this case the commercial banks that belong to the Federal Reserve System. Also similar to a GSE, the federal government backs the obligations of the Federal Reserve System, in this case, the Federal Reserve notes that circulate as the currency of the United States.

On the other hand, since 1935 the Federal Reserve Board has had the attributes of a government agency.[14] Similar to a government agency, the president of the United States appoints the Federal Reserve chairman and the other governors of the Federal Reserve Board. Those governmentally appointed governors in turn are a majority of the Federal Open Market Committee, the important body that makes monetary policy in the United States. The case law that justifies the delegation of monetary policy to a mixed public-private board returns yet again to the precedent set in the Banks of the United States.[15]

Institutional Characteristics and Early U.S. Instrumentalities

This brief review of the early history of instrumentalities in the United States sheds light on important issues that still confront GSEs. First, the special charter alters and often reduces the impact of market forces on the private company. An instrumentality enters the market only after the government grants the charter; it serves only those market functions that the charter permits; and it generally ceases to exist only through government action in ending the charter.

The latter point gains special significance if the charter is tied to special government subsidies. An instrumentality such as the Union Pacific Railroad, which the government chartered in 1862 and rechartered in 1864, can succeed on the basis of government subsidies even if it might not otherwise be a commercial success. Conversely, a productive and commercially successful instrumentality such as the first Bank of the United States will go out of business if its charter ends.

Today a GSE such as the Federal Home Loan Bank System uses its government benefits to become a half-trillion dollar institution. Yet, with minor exceptions, the Federal Home Loan Banks serve virtually no purpose independent of the government subsidies that they allocate to their activities. Without the support of government, the Federal Home Loan Banks could probably not exist as functioning financial institutions in anything resembling their present form and size.

Second, political forces are more important than economic forces in determining the financial success of an instrumentality. The political strength of contending constituencies largely determines the value of the benefits and burdens that government includes in a charter.

Third, governments constantly adjust important elements of a charter. Those include the scope of authorized powers and markets as well as the amount of exaction (the "just and customary rents") to be paid in return for the privilege of a charter. Today the federal government makes constant adjustments to the charters of GSEs. The Federal Home Loan Bank System underwent changes in the 1980s that imposed virtual exactions on the GSE. Twice, in 1986 and 1989, the government assessed the Federal Home Loan Banks to help fund the savings and loan bailout and provide literally billions of dollars for the two financial assistance institutions, the Financing Corporation (FICO) and the Resolution Funding Corporation (REFCORP). One result of that government action was to discourage the Federal Home Loan Banks from maintaining reserves of retained earnings, for fear that government might seize them yet again.[16]

Finally, given the history of U.S. instrumentalities,[17] the federal government seems to have considerable latitude, as a matter of law, to make changes to the charters of GSEs. Thus, a court rejected a constitutional challenge and held that it was proper for Congress to enact legislation that required financially sound institutions of the Farm Credit System to contribute funds for the bailout of the system after it failed financially in the mid-1980s.[18]

Another court has held that "shareholders in Federal Home Loan Banks have no vested interest under the statute in the continued existence of a particular Federal Home Loan Bank or any legally protected private rights which would enable them to invoke the due process clause."[19] Congress has made this position explicit in a number of charter acts; the Fannie Mae charter act, for example, provides that the corporation shall have succession (that is, shall continue its corporate existence under the charter) until dissolved by an act of Congress.[20]

The Political Strength of Mercantilist Companies

Issues of political power are especially important to special-purpose companies. From mercantilist times, companies with special charter privileges have understood that their ultimate success or failure hinges even more on politics than on the efficient provision of services. Such companies have found it in their economic interests to gain substantial influence over the political process that provides them with access to valuable and often exclusive charter benefits. The intensity of such efforts can be understood only if one bears in mind the essential role of favorable legislation in ensuring the future prospects of an instrumentality. Conversely, adverse legislation can mean the end of an institution regardless of its position in the market.

Some mercantilist institutions, from the Bank of the United States in the nineteenth century to the thrift industry in the twentieth, have demonstrated their power. The most powerful instrumentality of its day, the second Bank of the United States, precipitated a depression in the early 1830s as a weapon in its war with President Andrew Jackson over rechartering. Historian Fritz Redlich writes of Nicholas Biddle, the president of the bank:

> When the bank war developed, Biddle proved to be a magnificent fighter. But, in view of his semi-official status, one may ask: Should he have fought as valiantly and as bitterly as he did? [H]e carried the fight to its extreme, and just as he did not recognize there were limits to be observed, he did not see when it was necessary to acknowledge defeat. ... [T]he struggle for a new charter became bitter war where power was pitched against power; where the end seemed to justify the means; where Biddle became more and more stubborn as it progressed; ... and for the first time in his life [he] became culpable: he abused the power which

he held in trust to engineer the depression of 1833/1834 in order to force his will on the administration and the country.[21]

Later in the nineteenth century, the Pacific Railway Commission found that the transcontinental railroads had exceeded their proper bounds in their drive for dominance:

It is the judgment of the Commission that money of all the bond-aided roads have been used for the purpose of influencing legislation. There is no direct proof, with specifications of time, place, and persons, on which to base the assertion that actual bribery was resorted to. But it is impossible to read the evidence of C. P. Huntington and Leland Stanford, and the Colton letters, without reaching the conclusion that very large sums of money have been improperly used in connection with legislation.[22]

More recently sheer political power helped much of the thrift industry stay alive in the 1980s despite the financial failure of hundreds of institutions. As late as 1986 and again in early 1987, the powerful U.S. League of Savings Institutions marshaled enough congressional support to stop legislation that would have provided funds for the insolvent federal deposit insurance fund so that it could pay to close failed savings and loan associations. Individual institutions were able to obtain the services of powerful members of the government to pressure regulators to keep their particular institutions open at great taxpayer expense long after they had failed.

GSEs follow a similar pattern to the other mercantilist institutions. The Farm Credit System wielded considerable political influence for many decades. Harold Seidman points to the system's achievement in 1953 of effective private ownership and control as a sign of the power of its constituency:

Farm organizations . . . convinced President Eisenhower to support legislation that provided independent financing for the farm credit system and immunized it to effective federal control. Not all dependents were as successful as the farm credit organizations in gaining the four freedoms: freedom from financial control by the Congress, freedom from independent audit by the comptroller general, freedom from budget review by the president, and freedom to use federal funds.[23]

For decades, the board members of FCS institutions found a favorable reception at the congressional agriculture committees and other committees where rural lawmakers were influential.[24] Even after the FCS announced in 1985 that it could not meet its obligations, rural members of Congress persisted in protecting the cooperative FCS shareholders from the financial consequences.[25]

In the process of enacting the 1992 legislation to set effective capital standards and create meaningful financial supervision for Fannie Mae and Freddie Mac, the two companies exerted considerable influence over the House Banking Committee, both directly and through their dominance of third parties. As Representative Jim Leach, the committee's sole dissenter, reported:

> It is not surprising that Fannie and Freddie are beginning to exhibit that arrogant characteristic of a duopoly, controlling 90 percent of the market. Such market dominance allows for heavy-handed approaches to competitors, to financial intermediaries, and to consumers. Competitors such as community based savings and loan associations and commercial banks are also users of GSE services. They are understandably apprehensive about expressing reservations about their practices in fear of retaliation. Likewise, would-be competitors such as securities firms run well known market risks if they object or attempt to compete with Fannie and Freddie. The two GSEs distribute billions of dollars of business on Wall Street and have a reputation of not cottoning to challengers of the status quo.[26]

When the *Economist* of London published a series of articles that the GSEs perceived as unfavorable, and also a cartoon (figure 5-1), Fannie Mae first complained and then withdrew its advertising account.[27]

A review of some news headlines from the *Wall Street Journal*, the *New York Times*, and other sources gives the flavor of the determination with which GSE may try to hold on to its charter privileges:

- "Inquiry into Fannie Mae Pressure," *New York Times*, May 4, 1983, p. D1

FIGURE 5-1

"Uncle Sam Sends Them Next Door"

- "Debate on New U.S.-Backed Mortgage Security Stirs Charges of Greed, Government Domination," *Wall Street Journal*, April 20, 1987, p. 48
- "Power of the Mortgage Twins: Fannie and Freddie Guard Autonomy," *New York Times*, November 12, 1991, p. D1
- "Powerful Corporation Persuades House Panel to Retreat on Tax," *New York Times*, June 24, 1993, p. A18
- "The Money Machine: How Fannie Mae Wields Power," *Washington Post*, January 16, 1995, p. A1
- "A Medici with Your Money: Fannie Mae's Strategic Generosity," *Slate*, February 22, 1997
- "HUD to Query Fannie Mae on Underwriter's Withdrawal from Freddie Mac Debt Deal," *Inside MBS & ABS*, May 28, 1999
- "AEI Conference on Fannie, Freddie Spawns Crossfire," *Dow Jones Newswire*, September 9, 1999
- "Fannie Mae Hit on Lobbying Bid: 2 Lawmakers Criticize Letter Campaign," *Washington Post*, May 17, 2000, p. E3
- "Firms Report Fannie Mae, Freddie Mac Threats," *Wall Street Journal*, March 8, 2001, p. A3

That attitude, backed by the immense resources available to a GSE, results in a political environment that the GSE tends to dominate. In 1996 the Treasury Department reported on the difficulty of adjusting GSE charter acts to take account of changing public priorities:

> When creating a GSE, Congress defines the problem (i.e., the market imperfection) it seeks to overcome, provides benefits (subsidies), and imposes limitations on the GSE. But if Congress wishes to revise those decisions in response to changing public needs, it no longer has the same freedom of action. In addition to the usual constraints of the legislative process, it must contend with the private interests of the GSE and its shareholders. Congress must consider, and legislate, any such changes through a process in which the GSEs are significant participants. As a private company, the GSE will act to fulfill its fiduciary responsibilities by promoting and protecting the interests of its shareholders.[28]

Indeed the Treasury Department itself came under intense GSE pressure in writing its 1996 report, to the point that the department

TABLE 5-1
LOBBYING EXPENDITURES IN 1998

Fannie Mae and Freddie Mac (combined)	$7,710,000
National Association of Realtors	6,040,000
American Bankers Association	4,645,000
Bond Market Association	2,591,000
America's Community Bankers	2,290,000
Mortgage Insurance Companies of America	1,560,000
National Association of Home Builders	940,000

SOURCE: *Inside Mortgage Finance.* "Fannie, Freddie Lobbying Spending Jumps Significantly in 1999, Latest Filings Reveal," *Inside Mortgage Finance,* December 10, 1999.

substantially weakened its proposed statements about desirability and feasibility of removing government sponsorship from Fannie Mae and Freddie Mac.[29] More recently, in response to growing controversy about their role in the mortgage market, Fannie Mae and Freddie Mac have increased their already substantial presence in the political process. Table 5-1 shows how the combined lobbying expenditures of Fannie Mae and Freddie Mac in 1998 exceeded those of trade associations of other traditional participants in the housing markets, including real estate brokers, homebuilders, mortgage bankers, and even commercial bankers and thrift institutions.[30] In 1999 Fannie Mae and Freddie Mac increased their combined spending on lobbying to more than $11 million in response to growing political activity by private mortgage market companies seeking to limit the expansion of the two GSEs and greatly increased their so-called soft money political contributions.[31] Such political strength does have its limits, especially if a GSE falters or fails. Nonetheless these institutions tend to be powerful enough to make government supervision, and even the enactment of appropriate protective legislation, difficult at best.[32]

The Different Behavior of Instrumentalities

Mercantilist companies are different from ordinary companies. They may provide valuable public benefits but lack some of the basic forms of market discipline that apply to the usual company chartered under state business corporation laws. The mercantilist charter means that the contest among financial competitors too often occurs in a political forum rather than in the marketplace.

A review of the history of mercantilist institutions reveals a pattern. First, a government establishes one or more instrumentalities under a favorable charter, often including exclusive privileges. Then the government helps the instrumentality to protect its monopoly or other position in the marketplace. The instrumentality often obtains expansions of its legislated charter powers.

The expansionary phase is followed by an increase in opposition from competitors and other powerful interests. That opposition, as with the Farm Credit System today, can sometimes confine the instrumentality and prevent expansion of charter powers. But too often some form of political risk (dramatically seen in the actions of the Federal Reserve Board that helped to drive much of the thrift industry into insolvency within two years, from 1979 to 1981), can call the future of an instrumentality into question. Then comes, as with the thrift industry, political pressure on regulators and the government to forebear rather than to close the institutions. Finally, some crisis may make the status quo untenable.

Through the progression, instrumentalities may provide significant public services, often over decades, that the government might not have provided as well through its own agencies. However, the pace of change in the marketplace, and especially the financial marketplace, has accelerated. That acceleration means a significant increase in the speed with which the markets erode the charter advantages of an instrumentality. Such erosion decreases the public benefits that such companies may be able to offer and increases their financial vulnerability.

Many kinds of risk that can topple those institutions can be qualitatively different from those that affect other companies. They may be inherently nonquantifiable. Thus rapid advances in technology create the prospects of unforeseen erosion of the market share of a company confined to a special-purpose charter. Instrumentalities have quite different market risk from other companies. They may enjoy oligopoly profits undisturbed for years, only to be confronted suddenly with new technologies that permit aggressive competitors to emerge and rapidly take away key portions of their customer base.

As with other companies, management and operations risks of a financial instrumentality may depend on new technologies. Unlike ordinary companies, the management risk of a financial instrumentality may jump dramatically when it runs into the limits of its enabling legislation and managers feel themselves forced to take greater risks within their permitted markets.[33]

Such risks, and other new types of risks that emerge when institutions and their managers become stressed, are largely nonquantifiable, at least until after they have caused large-scale financial damage. Perhaps the greatest of the nonquantifiable risks is political risk. As cases of failing thrifts and banks have shown, the government can be slow to respond to early warning signals of financial distress. Moreover, the political process reveals a tendency to compound those risks rather than to contain them promptly.

In summary, the enabling legislation governing most general-business corporations reflects the democratic process in response to events over the past two hundred years. Today groups of incorporators can form and dissolve most companies with relative ease. However, among the great majority of corporations chartered under general-corporation laws of the states remains a minority of companies chartered with distinctive privileges and restricted activities and powers. Government-sponsored enterprises manifest behavior that can be understood only in terms of their mercantilist origins.

6

The Consequences of Organizational Form and Governance: A Case Study of the Housing GSEs

The functions of an organization primarily dictate the appropriate form for its structure. At the same time the selection of a particular structure can have a substantial impact on the activities of the organization. In those respects Fannie Mae and Freddie Mac provide an interesting counterpoint to the Federal Home Loan Bank System. The contrast between the dynamic and innovative Fannie Mae and Freddie Mac and the generally outmoded Federal Home Loan Bank System relates in good part to the fact that Fannie Mae and Freddie Mac are investor-owned and shareholder-controlled while member-borrowers own and cooperatively govern the Federal Home Loan Banks.

Today all three housing GSEs are privately owned and operate with boards of directors that include a minority of members appointed by the government. They each are secondary mortgage market facilities but by law provide somewhat different financial services. As discussed in chapter 3, the GSEs benefit from special government privileges, including the ability to borrow great volumes of money less expensively than warranted by their creditworthiness alone, if considered without regard to their ties to the government. Their special privileges have helped to make Fannie Mae, Freddie Mac, and the Federal Home Loan Bank System some of the largest financial institutions in the United States, each holding housing-related assets amounting to hundreds of billions of dollars or more.

To see how their governance structure affects financial performance, consider first the way that principles of fiduciary responsibility lead officers and directors of GSEs to serve the interests of owners and then consider the contrast in governance and institutional behavior between the Federal Home Loan Bank System and Fannie Mae.

The Fiduciary Responsibilities of
GSE Officers and Directors

The officers and directors of a corporation have a fiduciary responsibility to the company and to shareholders. That responsibility is the starting point for understanding the implications of governance structures for the behavior of corporations and other types of institution with officers and directors who make decisions that affect other people's investments.

As a general rule, the purpose of an investor-owned company is to make profits for its shareholders.[1] The principle does not change when an investor-owned company is an instrumentality of a government.[2] An investor-owned company must justify any participation in benevolent activities in terms of shareholder benefit. Well-established law dictates that the management of an investor-owned company may not divert significant amounts of the shareholders' money to purposes other than profitable activities.[3] David Maxwell, Fannie Mae's former chairman, once explained the company's low-income housing initiatives in terms of the GSE's shareholders: "Remember, we don't do this as a charity. We make money doing these things. I'm not hired to give away stockholders' money."[4]

The legal rights of shareholders are enforceable in court. Directors and officers of an investor-owned instrumentality are subject to personal liability for breaching their fiduciary duties.[5] The GSEs reinforce the identification of their directors and officers with the interests of shareholders by offering generous stock-option plans.

The authority of GSE directors and officers relates to the extent that a government regulator may intervene in the internal corporate affairs of the GSE. Thus, when the Federal Home Loan Bank Board governed Freddie Mac, that board of three federal officials had the authority to require the GSE to engage in financial transactions to the potential detriment of the financial soundness of the GSE. By contrast, the legislative history of the Fannie Mae Charter Act of 1968 specifies that

> it is the intent of the Committee that the regulatory powers
> of the Secretary will not extend to FNMA's internal affairs,
> such as personnel, salary, and other usual corporate mat-
> ters, except where the exercise of such powers is necessary
> to protect the financial interests of the Federal Government
> or as otherwise necessary to assure that the purposes of the
> FNMA Charter Act are carried out.[6]

The legislative history of Freddie Mac's restructuring with the demise of the Federal Home Loan Bank Board in 1989 contains similar
expressions of congressional intent.

Both the Federal Home Loan Bank System and the Farm Credit
System have needed to disentangle themselves from their earlier
close relationship with their government regulators. Congress enacted legislation in 1985 and again in 1987 to create more of an arm's-
length relationship between the Farm Credit System institutions and
their regulator, the Farm Credit Administration. The FCA states that
FCS directors have fiduciary responsibilities: "Directors [of an FCS
institution], like other corporate directors, owe fiduciary duties to
the institution and must exercise reasonable care in governing the
institution's activities."[7]

The FCA has issued regulations that set standards of conduct
for FCS directors and employees.[8] Those standards attempt to deal
with special issues of governance in the unusual cooperative structure of the FCS. For example, directors of an FCS institution must be
borrowers from that institution; in the view of FCA, that relationship creates a need to deal explicitly with the fact that insider transactions are more prevalent than for an investor-owned financial
institution.

The Federal Housing Finance Board has not gone as far in creating an arm's-length relationship with the Federal Home Loan
Banks. However, it too has issued regulations to spell out the fiduciary responsibility of the directors of the Federal Home Loan Banks:

> The Finance Board believes that, attendant to the exercise of
> customary and useful corporate powers, the Banks' boards
> of directors are subject to the same general fiduciary duties
> of care and loyalty to which the board of a state-chartered
> business or banking corporation would be subject, although
> this previously has not been set forth in regulation.[9]

The directors and officers of all GSEs have a fiduciary responsibility to act in the best interests of the institution and its owners. For investor-owned GSEs, the owners are investors; for the cooperative GSEs, the owners are borrowers or other users of the GSE's financial services.

The Tension between Public Purpose and Private Profits

Several observers have commented on "the tension between profit and public purpose."[10] The government has not been especially successful either at attempting to improve GSE service to public purposes or at reducing the public's risk exposure from GSE activities. According to a report of the Congressional Budget Office on Fannie Mae and Freddie Mac, "the balance of incentives appears to favor shareholders strongly at the expense of taxpayers and the public interest."[11]

Two examples illustrate the problem. The first relates to the federal efforts to ensure that Fannie Mae and Freddie Mac provide access to the mortgage market for underserved borrowers and communities; the second relates to the growth of Freddie Mac's portfolio to today's immense size despite the increased exposure of the public to risks from that funding strategy and an express commitment from Freddie Mac to the Congress not to do so.

Affordable Housing Goals. The 1992 Federal Housing Enterprises Financial Safety and Soundness Act directs HUD to establish numeric housing goals that require Fannie Mae and Freddie Mac to purchase mortgages that serve targeted groups. The act requires HUD to set three types of goals:

- housing for low- and moderate-income families;
- housing located in central cities, rural areas, and other underserved areas; and
- special affordable goals that target very low-income and low-income families living in low-income areas.

HUD periodically issues weak regulations to set goals for Fannie Mae and Freddie Mac. HUD has informed Congress that its analysis of so-called HMDA data, collected pursuant to the Home Mortgage Disclosure Act,[12] shows that both GSEs continue to lag the rest of the market in funding affordable housing loans for lower-income families and in underserved communities:

Fannie Mae and Freddie Mac have been successful in meeting their housing goal requirements in the past, yet their share of the affordable housing market is substantially smaller than their share of the total conventional conforming market. Lower income families, certain minorities, central-city residents, and immigrant populations continue to be underserved by Fannie Mae and Freddie Mac.[13]

HUD also reported that the GSEs were extremely cautious in serving the affordable housing market: "A large percentage of the lower-income loans purchased by both GSEs have relatively high down payments, which raises questions about whether the GSEs are adequately meeting the needs of lower-income families, who find it difficult to raise enough cash for a large down payment."[14]

An earlier GAO report concluded with an observation similar to HUD's that "the enterprises continue to trail the primary market" in most categories of service to targeted groups and locations.[15] Table 6-1 shows the most recent available data at the time (for 1996) used by GAO.[16]

Despite their access to substantial government benefits, the GSEs did not manage to outperform the rest of the private market in service to those homebuyers and communities that most need public support. The government, especially when acting through the Department of Housing and Urban Development, has not been successful at inducing Fannie Mae and Freddie Mac to allocate more government subsidies away from shareholders as a means even of

TABLE 6-1
FANNIE MAE, FREDDIE MAC, AND AFFORDABLE HOUSING

Borrower Group	% of Fannie Mae Mortgage Purchases	% of Freddie Mac Mortgage Purchases	% of Primary Market Originations
Very low income	8.6	8.0	10.8
African-American	4.4	3.6	4.7
Underserved areas	21.3	18.9	23.3

SOURCE: General Accounting Office, *Federal Housing Enterprises: HUD's Mission Oversight Needs to Be Strengthened*, GAO/GGD-98-173 (Washington, D.C.: GAO, July 1998), table 3.1, p. 58.

matching the performance of private lenders in support of afford-able housing for targeted groups.

Building a Huge Portfolio. A financial institution such as a GSE can fund mortgages either through securitization, that is, by issuing or guaranteeing mortgage-backed securities, or by holding the mort-gages in portfolio. Economists have long observed that the GSE pur-chase of mortgages for their portfolios provides a transitory benefit at best; they have suggested that public benefits would be increased by eliminating that form of arbitrage in favor of GSE funding through mortgage-backed securities. Funding through a portfolio adds to a GSE's exposure to interest rate risk compared with funding through mortgage-backed securities.[17]

The choice of funding activity tends to reflect the interests of a GSE's owners rather than concern for public policy. For years Freddie Mac declined to grow a large mortgage portfolio that might com-pete with the interests of its thrift institution owners. Instead Freddie Mac securitized mortgages in ways that would complement the in-terests of its owners by swapping their whole loans for mortgage-backed securities that they continued to hold in portfolio.

In 1989 Freddie Mac Chairman Leland Brendsel testified to Congress on the value of that approach:

> Since inception since 1970 Freddie Mac has had the same strategy, a business strategy of avoiding interest rate risk. . . . This strategy was started by its founders back in 1970, continued on by my predecessors, and I carry on that tradition today.
>
> We avoid interest rate risks by financing about 95 per-cent of all the mortgages we purchase with mortgage backed securities. . . . As a result we are insulated largely from the squeeze on earnings experienced by most deposi-tory institutions when interest rates rise.[18]
>
> Chairman Pickle [Rep. J.J. Pickle, D-TX]: "How much extra interest risk would it pose if you began a large port-folio in your lending program? . . . What would prevent Freddie Mac, then, from becoming a large portfolio lender, anything? Yes, what?"
>
> Mr. Brendsel: "Me, the board of directors. Let me men-tion again —"
>
> Chairman Pickle: "'Me' is not 'the law.'"

Mr. Brendsel: "No, I understand Mr. Chairman. The mission of the corporation is to increase the availability and the affordability of mortgage money. . . . In order to do that, we must operate in a safe and sound manner."[19]

When Brendsel made his commitment, Freddie Mac's portfolio at year-end 1988 amounted to about $16.9 billion compared with outstanding mortgage-backed securities of $226.4 billion. Ten years later, at the end of 1998, Freddie Mac's portfolio had grown to $256 billion compared with outstanding mortgage-backed securities of $478 billion. Freddie Mac's retained portfolio then amounted to more than one-third of its total activities, or about seven times the 5 percent ratio that Brendsel had promised the Ways and Means Committee. Freddie Mac's portfolio continues to grow each quarter.

A major factor in that change was probably the company's change in governance structure. Until 1989 the three federal officials who constituted the Federal Home Loan Bank Board governed Freddie Mac. Members of the bank board tended to have close ties to the thrift industry that until the late 1980s also owned (directly or indirectly) all stock in Freddie Mac. Just about the time that Brendsel testified, Freddie Mac converted to investor ownership and a shareholder-controlled board of directors with fiduciary responsibility to the investor shareholders of Freddie Mac. Stock analysts regularly value the stock of Fannie Mae and Freddie Mac according to the extent that the portfolio is expected to grow.[20] The new directors undoubtedly saw growing Freddie Mac's portfolio as a way to increase earnings regardless of the increased risk to the government.

For all GSEs the interests of the institution and its owners come first as a matter of both law and practical reality in the minds of GSE officers and directors. Despite the common responsibility of a GSE's leadership, a cooperative structure leads to quite different institutional behavior from an investor-owned GSE, as this case study illustrates. Consider first the Federal Home Loan Bank System, a cooperative, and then Fannie Mae, an investor-owned company.

The Federal Home Loan Bank System

The Federal Home Loan Bank System consists of twelve regional banks that provide collateralized loans, called *advances*, to member–financial institutions. Originally the Federal Home Loan Bank Act limited membership in the bank system generally to savings and loan associations. In 1989, after the savings and loan debacle greatly diminished the number of thrift institutions, Congress expanded the system's charter to provide for membership by other institutions, especially commercial banks with significant mortgage portfolios, and set a new regulator of the Federal Home Loan Banks, the Federal Housing Finance Board (FHFB), an independent government agency.

The governance structure of each Federal Home Loan Bank includes a president-CEO and a fourteen-member board of directors. The board consists of eight shareholder-elected directors and six directors who are appointed by the FHFB. By law at least two of the appointed directors must be consumer representatives. The FHFB designates each elected director as representing members of a particular state included in the district served by the bank.[21]

The Federal Home Loan Banks have traditionally provided their primary benefit in the form of collateralized loans to members that choose to borrow from the system. Because of their GSE status, the Federal Home Loan Banks can offer longer maturity advances than may otherwise be available to members. The primary benefit of bank advances is the ready source of liquidity that members can tap at times of need. Advances also allow members to fund their mortgage portfolios with borrowings of comparable duration. The banks provide other services for their members such as data processing and trustee services.

In earlier decades, Federal Home Loan Bank advances could be essential to the savings and loan industry. When the law limited thrifts to serving local market areas, the Federal Home Loan Bank System used its status as a GSE to borrow money in cash-rich areas and provide those funds to local savings and loan institutions making mortgages in developing but cash-poor parts of the country. In the 1960s the law imposed ceilings on the interest rates that thrifts could pay for deposits. When interest rates rose, deposits flowed out of thrift institutions in a process known as *disintermediation*. At such times Federal Home Loan Bank advances provided a much-needed source to help thrift institutions to fund their mortgage portfolios.

Today members see the bank advance as merely one source of funds among many. The high collateral requirements to receive a bank advance often make other sources more attractive. Indeed many members buy stock in a bank as a way to receive dividends rather than to receive advances.

The governance structure of the banks helps to ensure that they support rather than compete with their members. One president-CEO of a large member-bank explains privately that the governance structure includes directors who are reelected to serve long terms, plus a rotating series of president-CEOs. While the pattern for other banks may vary, clearly the tenure of a bank president-CEO depends directly on the satisfaction of members with the quality of service from that bank.

Thus the Federal Home Loan Banks have been reluctant even to consider charter expansions, for example, to guarantee mortgage-backed securities, that might interfere with the profits of their members. Over time, as the role of bank advances has declined in importance, such charter expansions have seemed increasingly needed if the banks were to continue to be relevant to today's dynamic mortgage market. At the end of 1995 the Federal Home Loan Banks together held an investment portfolio, largely unrelated to any public purpose, that exceeded the total volume of advances outstanding. The ratio has declined somewhat in recent years.

The FHFB and Congress have been seeking new missions and functions for the bank system. The Gramm-Leach-Bliley Act of 1999 permits banks to offer advances to their smaller members that are collateralized by small business loans, agriculture, and rural and community development loans, not merely home mortgages. The act removes limits on the extent that advances may be collateralized by commercial real estate. It is not clear that the overcollateralized advance, even as the types of eligible collateral are expanded, can long remain a competitive product in today's financial environment. The problem once again is capital: to obtain an advance, the member–financial institution must bear the burden of capital requirements imposed at two levels, both for the bank that provides the advance and for the member-institution that receives it.

Even without obtaining legislation, the Federal Home Loan Bank of Chicago has developed a new mortgage-funding program that may become a substitute for traditional advances. The new program, known as Mortgage Partnership Finance and described in chapter 4, allows a lender that is a member of a Federal Home Loan Bank to originate mortgages funded directly by the Federal Home Loan Bank on the basis of its access to low-cost GSE funding. In contrast to the traditional advance, the program requires that capital be set aside by the bank that funds the mortgages, not by the lender that originates those mortgages for the program. Other Federal Home Loan

Banks have followed with their own versions of the program. Before the Mortgage Partnership Finance program grows to a significant scale, it must overcome some operational obstacles.

Community bankers and others have sought to expand the lending authority of the Federal Home Loan Banks in other ways. It is not clear that most Federal Home Loan Banks could handle the credit risk inherent in expanded powers. The banks and their managers generally lack the capacity to underwrite loans. The result could be similar to the costly experience of some thrift institutions under the Garn-St Germain Act of 1982 after they left the sheltered environment of tight government regulation to enter new competitive markets. Coming from a tightly regulated environment with a limited product, the banks may be enticed to enter new markets, such as the markets for agricultural, rural, and small business loans, where both competitors and customers will eagerly send them the worst loans. Such changes in the functions of the Federal Home Loan Banks would also require substantial enhancement of government supervision of their safety and soundness.

Fannie Mae and Freddie Mac

Fannie Mae and Freddie Mac provide an interesting contrast to the Federal Home Loan Banks. From its inception in 1938 until 1968, Fannie Mae served the secondary mortgage market as a federal government agency. Its charter permitted Fannie Mae to purchase (but not originate) and sell residential mortgages insured by the Federal Housing Administration or guaranteed by the Veterans' Administration.

Fannie Mae was a secondary mortgage market facility for lenders throughout the nation. Especially in its early years, mortgage bankers used Fannie Mae's services; thrift institutions preferred to hold mortgages in portfolio rather than selling them to Fannie Mae.

Even as a government agency, Fannie Mae was able to use its market position to promote innovations in the residential mortgage market. For example, Fannie Mae helped to promote the use of title insurance as a way to reduce dependence on outmoded title registration and transfer systems.

In 1968 the federal government found itself compelled to deal with growing federal budget deficits. That year the Johnson administration proposed to sell Fannie Mae as a corporation to private shareholders as a way to raise money. The government would separate the secondary market functions into those that were profitable, to be carried out by a new private company, and those that were not profitable, to be carried out by a new government agency as the Government National Mortgage Association (Ginnie Mae).[22]

Originally the Johnson administration considered a cooperative structure for Fannie Mae, in part to ensure that private parties would be willing to pay for sufficient stock in the new company. The administration's final proposal structured the company as investor-owned but with a statutory provision for stock purchases by mortgage companies that sold mortgages to the company or serviced them. The board of directors consisted of a majority of shareholder-elected directors and a minority of directors appointed by the president of the United States.

The cooperative vestiges of the early thinking about the 1968 proposal can be seen in the statutory requirements that at least one of the appointed directors come from the homebuilding industry, at least one from the mortgage-lending industry, and at least one from the real estate industry. In practice the requirements have been useful in strengthening ties between Fannie Mae and its constituent groups and in providing an aura of greater public purpose for the institution.

The sale of stock in the new company was a huge success. Fannie Mae's stock now trades on the New York Stock Exchange. As a government-sponsored enterprise rather than a government agency, Fannie Mae gained considerable flexibility in its operations. An early step was to reduce the number of employees inherited from the government agency; for the remaining employees, salaries rose significantly.[23]

In 1970 Congress created a parallel secondary mortgage company known as Freddie Mac, the Federal Home Loan Mortgage Corporation. The thrift industry pushed for the creation of Freddie Mac to complement the Home Loan Bank System in supporting thrift institution activities through the secondary mortgage market.[24]

Initially Freddie Mac's board of directors consisted of the three government officials who were members of the government agency responsible for oversight of the thrift industry, the Federal Home Loan Bank Board. As government officials with limited compensation, the Federal Home Loan Bank Board tended to hold down compensation of Freddie Mac officials and employees to similar levels. A consequence of the difference in governance structures between Fannie Mae and Freddie Mac was that, especially in the 1980s, Fannie Mae's compensation packages tended to exceed those of Freddie Mac. Fannie Mae used the disparity to attract talent from its rival.

By 1970 the growth of the private mortgage insurance industry meant that Congress was ready to expand Fannie Mae's charter authority. Both Fannie and Freddie were permitted to deal not only in government-insured or guaranteed mortgages but also in those backed by private mortgage insurance. Today Fannie Mae and Freddie Mac can deal in investment-grade conventional (that is, privately insured) mortgages up to a level specified by statutory formula based on new house prices each year.

Fannie Mae and Freddie Mac have continued to push, often successfully, for the expansion of their charter authority. They also have used their market position to help improve the functioning of the secondary mortgage market. In 1971 the two companies, with congressional support, helped to standardize mortgage forms in the United States.[25] The two companies today are deploying innovative technologies to reduce transactions costs and improve service to the mortgage borrower. Automated underwriting systems of the two companies help to expand the availability of mortgages to people who might not have qualified under traditional standards of creditworthiness. The changes are evolving at an accelerating pace. A Freddie Mac analyst published a vision of a marketplace in which mortgages were completely integrated with other financial delivery systems.[26] Other financial institutions, which find themselves on the defensive in competition with Fannie Mae and Freddie Mac, have registered increasing concern.[27]

At the same time the enterprises have used their market power to build a base of political influence that resists government efforts to make any changes in their charters that management believes would not further the interests of the investor-shareholders.[28] The Congressional Budget Office reported in 2001 that Fannie Mae and Freddie Mac, today's largest GSEs, keep a significant portion of their public subsidies (worth about $10.6 billion to Fannie Mae and Freddie Mac in 2000) for shareholders rather than passing them on to homebuyers. In an earlier report the CBO pointed out that concern about the apparent imbalance between the costs and benefits of the housing GSEs extends beyond the $3.9 billion a year—37 percent of the total subsidy—that they retain:[29] "One further concern is that Fannie Mae and Freddie Mac rather than public officials substantially control the amount of subsidy provided to the GSEs."[30]

The investor-owned GSEs have gained so much power that their pursuit of investor returns may have begun to crowd out the public benefits. Their power also makes it difficult for the government to devise an exit strategy even if the public costs of all GSE activities, including more than $2 trillion of poorly supervised contingent liability for the government and taxpayers, begin to outweigh the public benefits.[31]

Governance Structure and the
Importance of Institutional Design

The contrast of Fannie Mae and Freddie Mac with the Federal Home Loan Bank System is instructive. Both GSEs have comparable access to federal subsidies, including the authority to borrow in the federal agency credit market. Yet the law provides for each GSE to undertake a completely different strategy for providing financial services.

From its beginnings as a government corporation, Fannie Mae served mortgage bankers that needed a secondary market institution to purchase the mortgages that they originated and serviced. As investor-owned companies, Fannie Mae and Freddie Mac have an incentive to use their federal subsidies to increase their profits within the limits that the political process will tolerate. The companies expand their lines of business, grow large portfolios, and maintain high leverage, all as ways to increase returns on equity. Until the 1990s at least, the mortgage banking industry welcomed expansions of Fannie Mae and Freddie Mac authority in those directions.

Managers of a Federal Home Loan Bank too have a fiduciary responsibility to the institution's owners. But the owners are the users of the institution's services. The institution thus gains an incentive to increase economic returns but only through activities that complement rather than compete with the interests of the user-owners. At least one Federal Home Loan Bank provides its advances to its members at rates below the actual cost of funds. The officers and directors of the bank view their responsibility as using the bank to support the interests of the owners rather than of reaping large benefits for the bank itself. Public benefits then become only incidental. The Congressional Budget Office found that the activities of the Federal Home Loan Banks led to only a minuscule lowering of home mortgage rates, amounting to about 3 basis points (0.03 percentage points) in 2000.[32]

The interests of the owners also prevail in the legislative process that determines the statutory authority that the Federal Home Loan Banks may exercise. The GSE will grow a large portfolio as a way to leverage its access to inexpensive federal credit. In contrast to Fannie Mae's and Freddie Mac's large mortgage portfolios, the Federal Home Loan Banks grow portfolios of nonmortgage investments. The banks traditionally refrained from growing large mortgage portfolios that might have competed with and reduced the returns of the portfolio lenders—banks and thrift institutions—that owned and controlled them. Now, because Fannie Mae and Freddie Mac dominate the conforming mortgage market, the Federal Home Loan Bank of Chicago has gained the latitude to compete in that market segment without being considered as infringing on the interests of the members of the Federal Home Loan Bank System.

Loyalty to user-owners is a critical reason why changes in governance can greatly alter the behavior of the institution. Cooperative owners do not want their GSE to compete with their profitability; that desire raises the specter of stagnation and increasing marginality for the GSE. By contrast investor-owners want the institution to use all its strength and the benefit of any available government subsidies to increase profits and shareholder returns, virtually without regard to potential effects on less subsidized competitors, even if those firms are part of the industry that sought creation of the GSE in the first place.

7
Changing Markets and Exit Strategies

As an instrumentality of government, a GSE involves a balance of public costs and public benefits. Similar to mercantilist institutions of old, a government charters a GSE to provide public benefits that it believes neither government nor the private sector otherwise might provide. As a matter of economics, the federal government chartered most GSEs to help overcome perceived market imperfections. The Office of Management and Budget suggests that "GSEs were created because wholly private financial institutions were believed to be incapable of providing an adequate supply of loanable funds at all times and to all regions of the country for specified types of borrowers."[1]

Markets evolve: at some point a GSE will have served the public purposes that lawmakers intended. The market imperfections that concerned policymakers may have resulted from legal impediments such as the now-repealed laws that limited banks and thrift institutions to serving narrow geographic areas. Or the impediments may have resulted from old ways of doing business that were superseded by the growth of dynamic private firms with access to improved technologies and business practices. In discussing the two largest GSEs, the Congressional Budget Office states:

> When the government turned to GSEs as a means of improving housing finance [in 1968 and 1970], no fully private firms could create profitable high-volume links between the bond markets and the mortgage markets. Today, numerous private groups can perform that service. . . . If the government eliminated the subsidy to Fannie Mae

and Freddie Mac, the mortgage markets would not retro-gress to pre-GSE condition. Rather, fully private interme-diaries, probably including Fannie Mae and Freddie Mac, would provide the funding links between markets. Improv-ing access to mortgage finance may have been a social ben-efit worth paying for in the past. It is now available without subsidy from fully private firms.[2]

New market developments may permit fully private firms, with-out government sponsorship, to serve many purposes that a GSE was originally chartered to serve. In economic terms the GSE then shifts from a function of helping to overcome market imperfections to helping to provide an off-budget subsidy to favored constituen-cies. The problem of obtaining public benefits commensurate with the costs is compounded when, as today, government has generally lost its ability to affect this balance.

The executive branch has several times stated its position on discontinuing federal sponsorship. The Treasury Department takes the following position: "The Treasury has for a number of years, in Democratic and Republican Administrations, believed that it is ap-propriate to wean a GSE from government sponsorship once the GSE becomes economically viable and successfully fulfills the pur-pose for which it was created with Federal sponsorship, or when the purpose for which it was created ceases to exist."[3] Similarly the Of-fice of Management and Budget states, "GSEs should only be cre-ated with a clearly articulated 'exit strategy' and an express sunset date in their charter."[4]

The GSE life cycle derives from the peculiar legal framework of GSEs, as discussed in chapter 2. A Sallie Mae privatization report raises the question, if government rather than the marketplace de-termines when a GSE finishes its work, when the GSE life cycle should end:

In creating the various GSEs, Congress did not contemplate the need at some point to unwind or terminate their fed-eral charters. However, Congress did not assume the per-petual existence (and continual expansion) of individual GSEs in the context of changing social and economic pri-orities. The missing element in the GSE concept is the no-tion of a life cycle for government sponsorship. GSEs are *created* to increase the flow of funds to socially desirable activities. If successful, they grow and *mature* as the market develops. At some point, the private sector may be able to meet the funding needs of the particular market segment. If so, a *sunset* may be appropriate.[5]

The question of setting such a sunset date then becomes a political matter rather than a policy issue.

The Difficulty of Designing an Effective Exit Strategy

Policymakers find it difficult to end government programs and even more difficult to terminate entire organizations.[6] The Reagan administration began, as David Stockman, its director of the Office of Management and Budget, explained, by searching out programs with weak claims for federal support. Instead the government acted primarily to terminate programs with weak constituencies.[7] More recently the House leadership in the mid-1990s sought to eliminate some government agencies and even an entire cabinet department. The efforts foundered, primarily because of a lack of political agreement that the government should withdraw from the activity that the agency or department carried out.

The efforts in the 1990s did close a handful of federal organizations that had been backed by weak constituencies. The agencies—the Office of Technology Assessment, the Advisory Commission on Intergovernmental Relations, and the Administrative Conference of the United States—read like a who's who of tiny organizations intended to improve the quality of governmental decisions without serving any particular constituency.

Ending the federal sponsorship of GSEs also can be difficult. The Reagan administration began its first term with bold statements from OMB about the desirability of removing federal sponsorship from the GSEs. Lawrence Kudlow, the associate director of OMB, testified in 1982 on legislation concerning Freddie Mac:

> The Administration believes that efforts should be made to better utilize FHLMC's first-rate management, solid marketing position, and positive earnings trend by seeking ways to sever all Federal government linkages with the agency [sic] within a specified interval, thus placing the corporation squarely in the private sector. This approach would be consistent with Administration policy to reduce all forms of federal and federally-assisted credit and to spin

off federally-related agencies into the private sector when-
ever possible. This approach would be consistent with
Administration objectives designed to strengthen the mar-
ket-oriented private economy as the most reliable instrument of sustained economic expansion.[8]

The administration believed that Fannie Mae and Freddie Mac
were ready to give up their GSE status. The Grace commission report on banking stated in 1983: *"Both FNMA and FHLMC want to
become fully private.* They would even be willing to give up the special advantages agency status offers in handling [MBSs] if they could
be reasonably assured of prospering in such an environment. However, for different reasons, they both fear losing agency status now."[9]

Only a few years later the administration's tone had changed to
one of complete frustration. In 1986 OMB Deputy Director Joseph
Wright wrote an objection to a speech in which David Maxwell, the
chairman and CEO of Fannie Mae, had criticized both the Reagan
administration and individuals on the White House staff who sought
to remove federal sponsorship from the GSE. Wright requested that
the Fannie Mae CEO "refrain from engaging in further distortions
of Administration policy in pursuit of the personal or other self-
interest that motivated [Mr. Maxwell's] statement to the Homebuilders."[10]

Instead of privatization of GSEs, the two terms of the Reagan
administration saw the failure and bailout of the Farm Credit System and the creation of a new GSE, Farmer Mac, essentially as the
political price that rural commercial banks demanded in return for
allowing Congress to enact the bailout legislation. Only the active
personal intervention of the secretary of the Treasury prevented
Congress in 1986 from creating yet another new GSE, to help fund
small businesses.[11]

The source of this political strength of GSEs relates to two inherent attributes of the GSE as a special type of instrumentality. First,
the government provides its primary subsidy to GSEs in the form of
implicit government backing that is not included as a part of the
federal budget. The imposition of new budget rules enabled the government, since the mid-1980s, to create constituencies in favor of
terminating, or at least reducing, many government programs. The
dynamics of a perceived zero-sum budget process meant that powerful constituencies developed in an attempt to take money from
other programs to help fund their own. By contrast the government
provides its subsidy to GSEs off budget and in a way that—so far at

least—has not been touched by budget rules. Some policymakers would be likely to object to the application of any budget rules to GSEs on the grounds of making the implicit government backing more explicit.

Second, as discussed in chapter 5, the GSEs have long understood that they must master the political process even more than the marketplace to protect themselves. They display a remarkable capacity to mobilize interested groups to rebuff efforts at even modest changes in their federal benefits. The *Washington Post* reported on Fannie Mae's use of market power to enlist political support: "Builders, real estate brokers and bankers across the country rely so heavily on Fannie Mae for mortgage funds that they live in fear of offending the firm and routinely defend it in Washington."[12]

A 1996 Congressional Budget Office report stated that various options existed for removing government sponsorship even from the largest GSEs without causing a disruption in the markets. The CBO added the caveat that the core issues might be political rather than technical:

> Of course, such options [to prepare for removal of government sponsorship] beg a question: why would the GSEs agree to those policies as a first step toward the withdrawal of their subsidy? That admission simply acknowledges that once one agrees to share a canoe with a bear, it is hard to get him out without obtaining his agreement or getting wet. If the GSEs were to support privatization, they and the Congress could certainly carry it out without financial disruption.[13]

In response to the CBO report, the two GSEs launched a campaign to discredit both the CBO and the analysts who had worked on the report.[14] While the creation of the perception of an implicit government guarantee may be a circumspect way to deliver an off-budget subsidy for a private instrumentality, the device can be difficult to wind down.

A Case Study: Removing Government Sponsorship from Sallie Mae

In 1996 Congress did enact legislation to remove government sponsorship from Sallie Mae.[15] The legislation is instructive from both the policy and the political perspectives. Consider the political process that led up to the 1996 law, the policy issues, and the mechanics of removing government sponsorship.

The Process Leading to the Act. The process leading to the 1996 act is important because of how it helped to create special incentives for Sallie Mae to support the end of government sponsorship. As a GSE, Sallie Mae returned substantial earnings to its owners, including returns on equity of more than 30 percent for many years. In the early 1990s both Congress and the Clinton administration began to consider the creation of a program of direct federal student loans to replace or at least substantially substitute for the existing guaranteed federal student loan program.

The change could have been a mortal blow to Sallie Mae as the largest single purchaser, holder, and servicer of federal guaranteed student loans. Unlike other commercial lenders, which would have shifted into other lines of business, its GSE charter prevented Sallie Mae from leaving the student loan business. Sallie Mae's CEO testified that if the federal government decided to move to a complete direct lending program in place of guaranteed loans, the most prudent course would be for the company to "liquidate its franchise."[16]

Congress created a second incentive for Sallie Mae to consider giving up its government sponsorship. The Omnibus Budget Reconciliation Act of 1993 contained a provision imposing an annual "offset fee" on Sallie Mae of 30 basis points (0.3 percent) of the GSE's holdings of federal student loans that the GSE acquired after the date of the new act.[17]

The offset fee had two effects. First, it neutralized much of the advantage that the GSE derived from borrowing in the federal agency debt market. Second, coming on the heels of the direct lending proposal, the imposition of the fee convinced the Sallie Mae leadership that the GSE's political risk was out of control.

Until the early 1990s Sallie Mae had been premier among GSEs in its ability to protect its franchise and extract valuable benefits from the political process; now company leaders seemed to feel as if potentially ruinous political risk had materialized. Being a purely private company would be much safer than continuing with the kind of political risk from a GSE charter that limited the company's ability to respond. Sallie Mae's CEO complained in testimony that between February 1993 and June 1996 the company had lost more than $4 billion in value for shareholders.[18]

Policy Issues. From a policy perspective the government needed to be certain that the removal of GSE status from Sallie Mae would not disrupt the student loan market. At the time of enactment of the legislation, Sallie Mae was seven times larger than its next competitor, the Student Loan Corporation, an institution established by Citibank, which owned 80 percent of it. According to one market analyst, Sallie Mae's share of the student loan market was "slightly larger than the mortgage market shares of Fannie Mae and Freddie Mac combined."[19]

The government also needed to pay attention to special parts of the student loan market. Because of the GSE's provision of letters of credit and other support to nonprofit student loan secondary market institutions and because of Sallie Mae's statutory role as an institution, the government could require the GSE to make loans of last resort to students who otherwise might not be able to obtain access to student loans.

The government addressed the issues through various devices. First, the student loan market was engaging in an increased process of securitization. Securitization, both by Sallie Mae and by other student loan institutions, was expected promptly to take up the slack left by any reduction in Sallie Mae's purchases of student loans. Second, the government had enacted legislation to create a direct student loan program that would allow an alternative source of student loan funds to take up much of the slack.

Third, the government might obtain the services of a lender-of-last resort, even without a GSE to provide them; "as the largest [student loan] financial participant regardless of its status, the privatized Sallie Mae will remain the obvious solution to this type of problem."[20]

Fourth, because Sallie Mae played a dominant role in the negotiations to give up its government sponsorship, the 1996 legislation allowed a leisurely transition. The act provided that Sallie Mae could not issue any GSE obligations with a maturity extending beyond September 30, 2008; the limitation would not apply to any debt issued to finance any lender-of-last-resort or secondary market purchase activity that the secretary of education might request. Sallie Mae negotiated an exit including immediate benefits of privatization (the authority to enter new lines of business), while winding down the company's GSE operations.

Mechanics. The statute created the following framework for privatization:[21]

1. The new law authorized the Sallie Mae board of directors to propose a reorganization plan that could involve the restructuring of Sallie Mae into a subsidiary of a holding company that would be authorized to create and operate other non-GSE subsidiaries (see figure 7-1).

2. The law required the Sallie Mae board to submit the restructuring plan to the shareholders; on approval of a majority of votes, the reorganization plan would go into effect.

3. The law set some limitations on the GSE. It may purchase student loans through September 30, 2007, but its other activities, such as the provision of warehousing advances and letters of credit and standby bond purchases, were restricted. The GSE must be wound up no later than September 30, 2008.

4. The law also set limitations on the non-GSE parts of the holding company and their relations with the GSE. The non-GSE parts are prohibited from acquiring student loans until the GSE is wound up. The holding company is prohibited from acquiring an interest in a financial institution[22] and must operate on an arm's-length basis from the GSE, although personnel may be shared. Only the GSE may use the name "Student Loan Marketing Association"; the non-GSE holding company may use the name "Sallie Mae" as a trademark and service mark, except in connection with an offering of debt or other securities.

5. The law strengthens the safety and soundness provisions applicable to the GSE.

6. The law requires the non-GSE holding company to issue to the District of Columbia Financial Responsibility and Management Assistance Authority stock warrants in an amount equal to 1 percent of the share value of the GSE just before the date of enactment of the law.

7. The law confers on the secretary of education certain authority, for example, to approve the termination of the GSE before September 30, 2008, and to require the holding company or any non-GSE part of the holding company to serve as a lender of last resort.

8. The law applies a sunset date to the GSE; even if shareholders do not approve the reorganization, the GSE shall dissolve and its separate existence shall terminate by July 1, 2013.

The mechanics of privatization have not been difficult. The law permits Sallie Mae's board to propose a simple reorganization to convert the GSE into a subsidiary of a non-GSE holding company. The basic change in structure is outlined in figure 7-1. The final winding up of the GSE's debt obligations is to be done through a transaction known as a *defeasance*: the organization irrevocably transfers sufficient funds or Treasury obligations to a trust and under the trust agreement ensures that the trustee will make full repayment of all liabilities on outstanding GSE obligations. Under GAAP rules a defeasance transaction permits the organization to remove all defeased liabilities from its balance sheet.

On July 31, 1997, Sallie Mae shareholders voted overwhelmingly to reorganize the company into a completely new entity according to the reorganization plan. Figure 7-1 schematically shows the new company just after reorganization. Sallie Mae also underwent a hard-fought proxy battle that resulted in the installation of new management for the reorganized institution. The new managers were led by former senior Sallie Mae officials who objected to the business plans put forth by the incumbents.

Some knowledgeable observers have concluded that

the privatization of Sallie Mae had little or no impact on the market which it served, raising the issue of whether Sallie Mae privatization should have been enacted several years earlier. Thus far, Sallie Mae's experience in the student loan marketplace immediately following the transition to privatization suggests that the company's GSE status was not crucial to liquidity in the student loan marketplace. . . . [This] raises the issue of whether the Sallie Mae GSE was allowed to retain its GSE status for long after it was serving a necessary or even beneficial function in the student loan marketplace.[23]

As a non-GSE, the new holding company can enter and leave lines of business without regard to the confines of a special-purpose charter act. The company has engaged in several acquisitions, including the purchase of two major firms, Nellie Mae, Inc., a major student loan origination company, and the USA Group, a major firm that specializes in guarantee servicing, student loan servicing, and secondary market operations. Sallie Mae has achieved vertical integration of its student loan business. The non-GSE has announced

FIGURE 7-1
Mechanics of Removing Government Sponsorship

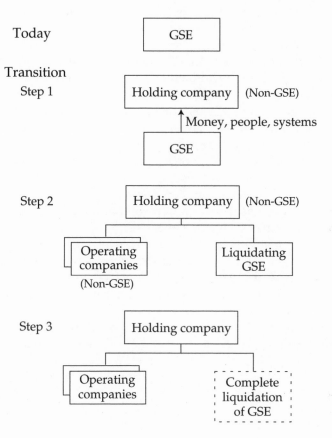

that it will team up with an insurance company to offer an array of insurance plans, including auto, home, life, and renters' insurance policies, annuities, prepaid legal services, and home warranty plans, to its 5 million student loan borrowers. The holding company has changed its name to USA Education, Inc., and projects about 6,500 employees and $1.4 billion in annual revenue.[24]

Lessons in Designing Exit Strategy

Several lessons emerge from the Sallie Mae experience and also from studies conducted by or for government agencies in 1994–1996.[25]

Mechanics. Given political support, the practical mechanics of surrendering government sponsorship can be addressed. An exit strategy, even for the largest GSEs, can be implemented without disruption to the market. The Sallie Mae privatization was made easier for the markets because of the availability of securitization as a way to fund student loans that Sallie Mae otherwise might have purchased as a GSE; in the home mortgage market securitization is even more developed as a means of funding large volumes of loans.

Fannie Mae and Freddie Mac do have a problem that Sallie Mae did not have to face. The two largest GSEs are so huge that the markets may perceive them to be too big to fail even if they lose their government sponsorship. Part of a solution may be a phase-in of bank-type capital standards before or while they begin to give up their government sponsorship. A natural result would then be to shrink the balance sheets of the two companies so that they lose some of their unnatural leverage and size.

The two GSEs with a cooperative structure also raise special issues about mechanics. One can envision a transition to investor ownership comparable to a mutual-to-stock conversion that many thrift institutions have implemented. Alternatively the institutions could shift charters completely. For example, some Farm Credit institutions may opt to adopt a credit union charter to maintain control in the hands of borrower-members. Other FCS institutions and some Federal Home Loan Banks may want to become commercial banks or thrift institutions. Given the cooperative governance of FCS institutions and Federal Home Loan Banks, some boards could opt to wind up their affairs and distribute as much of the institution's net worth to their members as permitted under the enabling legislation.

Incentives to Give Up GSE Status. From the perspective of GSE owners and managers, GSE status involves benefits, government subsidies, that must be weighed against costs, especially the prospect that the GSE charter sooner or later will confine their ability to respond effectively to more flexible competitors. GSEs develop and wield their political strength as a way to protect the value that comes with their GSE charter.

Over time, a GSE may serve a mature market. Fannie Mae and Freddie Mac may find that consumers demand more integrated financial services, such as so-called universal accounts, instead of the traditional home mortgage.[26] While the GSEs may be able to solve the problem partially with innovation such as providing portable mortgages and mortgages that include an embedded home equity line of credit,[27] at some point they may need to go further.

The limits of GSE status may become more pronounced for dynamic GSEs such as Fannie Mae and Freddie Mac than for others. Fannie Mae and Freddie Mac are transforming their strategic strength from the ability to provide low-cost funds to include more of an information-based capacity. Once they have that capacity, deploying it across a broad range of financial services might be profitable. By contrast some GSEs—the Federal Home Loan Banks are a striking example—actually provide little more than access to inexpensive federal agency credit.

GSEs are especially likely to consider giving up government sponsorship if they find themselves subject to serious political risk, as in the Sallie Mae example. Some GSEs may be subject to a type of political tipping point: either they are on top of the process, or the process suddenly turns extremely hazardous. Once the political environment turns ugly, a GSE may find its job of charter defense to be taxing at best. The perspective of GSE managers and corporate cultures also needs to be taken into account. Some GSE managers with a market orientation may relish the prospect of a new broad charter. Other GSE managers, with more political acumen than financial skills, may fear losing their jobs if the company loses its GSE status.

Finally, it must be understood that the GSEs themselves will play a major role in trying to influence the terms of any legislation to give up government sponsorship: "Although GSEs are the creation of Executive and Congressional action, any legislation to privatize or terminate a GSE is likely to be dominated by the GSE itself. Without a doubt, in the case of Sallie Mae the company's own lobbying throughout the privatization process substantially influenced the final version of the legislation."[28] For example, Sallie Mae obtained a much longer transition than the administration had wanted and also avoided a requirement to pay an explicit exit fee.

The Concerns of Stakeholders. Stakeholders must be assured that they will continue to thrive without a GSE. The housing industry may seek some new program or other substitute for the several billions of dollars of off-budget subsidy that the housing GSEs currently provide each year. The Department of Education sought to impose an exit fee on Sallie Mae as the price of letting the GSE give up its GSE status. Depending on the strength of constituencies other than the GSEs themselves, such an exit fee could be structured to benefit the public purposes, such as housing or agriculture, served by the congressional subcommittees that enact the legislation. In the end Sallie Mae avoided an express exit fee in exchange for (1) structuring the wind-down so that the 1993 offset fee would continue to be paid so long as GSE securities remain outstanding and (2) offering stock warrants to the District of Columbia Financial Control Board.

The concerns of stakeholders may be overblown, but they are real, especially for the largest of the GSEs, Fannie Mae and Freddie Mac. On the one hand the approximately $10.6 billion subsidy that the government delivered to housing (primarily homeowners) through the two GSEs in 2000 pales in comparison to the housing subsidies that government provides through the tax code. In 2000, for example, the government allowed $55 billion in home mortgage deductions, $19 billion in homeowner property tax deductions, and $19 billion in the exclusion of capital gains on home sales, plus billions of dollars in other tax subsidies such as the tax exemption on state and local bonds used to finance housing. The government spent another $24 billion that year in outlays for the Department of Housing and Urban Development and its programs.[29] In that context the $10.6 billion subsidy delivered through the two GSEs in 2000 would seem a relatively small part of the total amount of federal support for housing.

On the other hand homeownership is a cause close to the hearts of most Americans, and politicians would be foolhardy to disregard the issue. Perhaps the best approach is to create incentives for the GSEs themselves to favor the removal of government sponsorship, as in the Sallie Mae case. Then they become strong and powerful allies to help explain the need for privatization, rather than applying their formidable influence to try to undercut the legislation.

Another issue concerns affordable housing. The removal of government sponsorship would mean a more competitive mortgage market, which would reduce opportunities for cross-subsidization between more affluent borrowers and borrowers who need access to affordable housing. Fannie Mae and Freddie Mac have used their political power to resist being subjected to serious affordable housing requirements. Conversely the Federal Home Loan Banks contribute 10 percent of their earnings to an affordable housing fund that improves the ability of the market to serve borrowers that need special assistance. If the government removes its sponsorship from the Federal Home Loan Banks, exploring the creation of an alternative means of supporting affordable housing would be important. One option might be to create a new affordable housing fund that would be financed from a new offset fee imposed during the transition of the housing GSEs.

Alternatives to Full Privatization

Alternatives must be considered in the process of giving up government sponsorship. One option is simple inertia. Some GSEs and their managers may favor a straightforward continuation of the status quo for as long as possible. The tendency toward inertia has been especially pronounced in financial services legislation. Thus it took literally decades of effort before the government was able to enact broad financial reform legislation for commercial banks in 1999.

Today that alternative has serious drawbacks. The status quo is untenable in our fast-moving financial markets. The more dynamic GSEs will continue to grow and expand their activities. They will seek to maintain their hefty returns on equity even if the effort requires building huge portfolios and taking on other forms of financial risk.

The less capable GSEs will constantly seek new ways to make money. The Federal Home Loan Banks are especially at risk. At some point either the regulator or Congress is likely to enact changes in governance and permitted powers that would allow the Federal Home Loan Banks to undercut their own members. Perhaps most serious, the Federal Home Loan Banks have little experience in underwriting loans; as they move into new and untried activities, their financial risks could well turn into a serious risk for taxpayers.

A second alternative is more promising from a public policy perspective: continue the current GSE charters but reduce the amount of federal subsidy that they provide, especially in cases of financial failure. Congress essentially undertook that task in the FDIC Improvements Act of 1991 (FDICIA), in which it enacted safety and soundness reforms that reduced the potential costs to taxpayers of bank and thrift failures.

As discussed in chapter 4, the creation of an FDIC-type organization and an insurance fund to provide a cushion to pay for GSE financial failures would be an excellent first step. The creation of an insurance fund, financed through assessments on debt securities and MBSs issued by all GSEs, would help to supplement the capital that each GSE holds for itself. The application of some FDICIA reforms to GSEs at that step would help to protect taxpayers from having their money bail out a failed GSE, except under conditions similar to those established by FDICIA for a bailout of a failed commercial bank through the FDIC. With political will, the government could engineer such reforms without making the implicit government backing of GSEs any stronger than today.

Another interesting step might be to return to the intention of the 1934 act that first authorized the establishment of organizations such as Fannie Mae. At the time the entities were called *national mortgage associations*. A government regulator was authorized to charter and supervise multiple national mortgage associations, much as the Comptroller of the Currency charters national banks. The creation of many smaller GSEs to compete with Fannie Mae and Freddie Mac would help to reduce the inefficiencies associated with the monopoly power of the two GSEs. If combined with effective bank-type financial supervision and improved capital standards, the creation of competing national mortgage associations could help reduce the serious and imprudent concentration of financial risk that the government has created in the two trillion-dollar GSEs today.[30]

Several promising alternatives to the status quo exist. As with all issues relating to GSEs, the more intractable questions relate to the politics rather than the policies of designing a beneficial alternative to the status quo.

GSEs as Mercantilist Institutions in Modern Markets

For the moment at least, the existence of any natural checks on the process of GSE expansion is not clear. But it is instructive to turn once more to the history of earlier forms of mercantilist institutions. In particular the history of those institutions reveals a strong antipathy to the provision of special privileges to a government-sponsored company, especially to government-sponsored monopoly. Even in mercantilist times, special-purpose charters raised the issue of monopoly. [31] Those in a position to obtain a royal charter tried to obtain exclusive rights to carry on their business. Once a monopoly was granted, competitors came to the forefront of those objecting to the grant. The English East India Company provoked resentment among merchants in Great Britain[32] and in the American colonies. The tea dumped into Boston harbor in December 1773 belonged to the East India Company, which had the sole authority to import tea to the colonies.[33]

America has an intermittent tradition of strong antagonism against mercantilist companies. The early corporations were seen as monopolies and beneficiaries of special privilege; much of Andrew Jackson's message of veto of the charter of the Bank of the United States reflects that theme. Andrew Jackson's war on the Bank of the United States enjoyed widespread popular support in the 1830s, especially among the state banks that found themselves in competition with the national bank.

Later expressions of such resentment include Populist unhappiness with the monopoly behavior of the railroads and more recently the breakup of AT&T in the 1980s. In most cases the most vociferous opponents of government-sponsored companies came from firms that were forced to compete with the monopolies, not necessarily from consumers.

The GSEs today are subject to such resentment against their special privileges and monopolistic charters. Commercial banks opposed to Sallie Mae first proposed the offset fee that Congress imposed on that GSE in 1993 and that helped persuade Sallie Mae to give up its government sponsorship. The Farm Credit System finds itself kept in check by opposition from competing rural banks. A similar process of political discontent may be taking place toward the largest GSEs, Fannie Mae and Freddie Mac.[34]

GSEs were valuable instruments of government policy, especially in the first half of the twentieth century. The public benefits are now much less, and the actual and potential public costs are much greater. The transformation of resentment against monopoly into an effective political force may be the key to transforming GSEs into completely private companies. Ending the history of those instrumentalities on the positive note of their undoubted accomplishments would then be possible, rather than on a negative note of financial calamity or other public costs when they come to the end of their life cycle.

Recommended Reading

Those who wish to study GSEs further may want to consult the following studies:

Congressional Budget Office. 1991. *Controlling the Risks of Government-Sponsored Enterprises*. Washington, D.C.: Government Printing Office.
———. 1996. *The Public Costs and Public Benefits of Fannie Mae and Freddie Mac*. Washington, D.C.: Government Printing Office.
Department of Housing and Urban Development. 1996. *Studies on Privatizing Fannie Mae and Freddie Mac*. Washington, D.C.: Government Printing Office.
Office of Federal Housing Enterprise Oversight. 1995–2000. *Report to Congress*. Washington, D.C.
Stanton, Thomas H. 1991. *A State of Risk*. New York: HarperCollins.
———. 1991. "Federal Supervision of Safety and Soundness of Government-Sponsored Enterprises." *Administrative Law Journal* 5 (2) (summer): 395–484.
Wallison, Peter J., ed. 2001. *Serving Two Masters, Yet Out of Control*. Washington, D.C.: AEI Press.

Notes

Preface

1. Harold Seidman, *Politics, Position, and Power*, 5th ed. (New York: Oxford University Press, 1998).

2. Fannie Mae serves the secondary mortgage market in a quite different manner than if it had continued as a wholly owned government corporation and a part of the federal government. See Thomas H. Stanton and Ronald C. Moe, "Government Corporations and Government-Sponsored Enterprises," in Lester M. Salamon, ed., *The Tools of Government: A Guide to the New Governance* (New York: Oxford University Press, forthcoming).

3. For one example, see the testimony of Thomas H. Stanton before the U.S. Senate, Committee on Banking, Housing, and Urban Affairs, *The Safety and Soundness of Government Sponsored Enterprises*, Senate hearing 101-523. 101st Congress, 1st session, October 31, 1989, p. 41 (pointing out that increases in the stringency of capital requirements and government supervision for thrift institutions would drive billions of dollars of mortgages out of the portfolios of savings and loan associations and into the secondary mortgage market, where capital standards and government oversight were much weaker).

4. For a variety of examples, see Salamon, supra, note 2.

5. Find at www.napawash.org/eom.

6. See Lester M. Salamon, ed., with Michael S. Lund, *Beyond Privatization: The Tools of Government Action* (Washington, D.C.: Urban Institute, 1989).

7. Ibid., p. 18.

8. When I published an earlier book about GSEs in 1991 *(A State of Risk)*, the *Economist* review (May 25, 1991, p. 98) chided me that I possessed "an (American) liberal's instinct that they [the GSEs] could be valuable instruments of federal policy in pursuit of wooly-sounding social goals."

Chapter 1: Mercantilist Institutions in the Marketplace

1. Adapted from Ronald C. Moe and Thomas H. Stanton, "Government Sponsored Enterprises as Federal Instrumentalities: Reconciling Private Management with Public Accountability," *Public Administration Review*, July–August 1989, pp. 321–29.

2. The Congressional Budget Act of 1974, as amended in 1990 (at 2 U.S.C. sec. 622 (8)), defines a government-sponsored enterprise as

a corporate entity created by law of the United States that —

(A) (i)   has a Federal charter authorized by law;
    (ii) is privately owned, as evidenced by capital stock owned by private entities or individuals;
    (iii) is under the direction of a board of directors, a majority of which is elected by private owners;
    (iv) is a financial institution with power to —
        (I)   make loans or loan guarantees for limited purposes such as to provide credit for specific borrowers or one sector; and
        (II) raise funds by borrowing (which does not carry the full faith and credit of the Federal government) or to guarantee the debt of others in unlimited amounts; and
(B) (i)   does not exercise powers that are reserved to the Government as sovereign (such as the power to tax or regulate interstate commerce);
    (ii) does not have the power to commit the Government financially (but it may be a recipient of a loan guarantee commitment made by the Government); and
    (iii) has employees whose salaries and expenses are paid by the enterprise and are not Federal employees subject to title 5 of the United States Code.

3. 12 U.S.C. secs. 2001–2279aa.

4. 12 U.S.C. secs. 1421–1449.

5. 12 U.S.C. secs. 1716–1723d.

6. 12 U.S.C. secs. 1415–1459.

7. 20 U.S.C. sec. 10872.

8. 12 U.S.C. sec. 2279aa.

9. The legal attributes of these institutions are discussed in Thomas H. Stanton, "Government Sponsored Enterprises: Another View," *Public Budgeting & Finance*, autumn 1989, pp. 81–86.

10. 12 U.S.C. sec. 1441.

11. 12 U.S.C. sec. 1441b.

12. Barbara Miles, "Government-Sponsored Enterprises: The Issue of Expansion into Mission-Related Business," Congressional Research Service, January 19, 1999, at p. CRS-4.

13. Department of Agriculture, Economic Research Service, *Agricultural Income and Finance: Situation and Outlook Report*, AIS-74 (Washington, D.C.: Government Printing Office, 2000), ap. table 1, p. 57.

14. Treasury, *Report of the Secretary of the Treasury on Government Sponsored Enterprises* (Washington, D.C.: Government Printing Office, May 1990), p. F-14. As late as 1997 the GSE continued to be about seven times the size of its next largest competitor, the Student Loan Corporation (Citibank owns 80 percent). Sanford Bernstein & Co., Bernstein Research, "Sallie Mae: Metamorphosis" (New York, October 1997), quoted in John E. Dean, Saul L. Moskowitz, and Karen L. Cipriani, "Implications of the Privatization of Sallie Mae," *Journal of Public Budgeting, Accounting & Financial Management* 11 (1) (spring 1999): 56–80, n. 35.

15. Office of Federal Housing Enterprise Oversight, *2000 Annual Report to Congress* (Washington, D.C.: OFHEO, 2000), pp. 10, 100, and 110.

16. One stock analysts' report notes that "the [GSEs'] charters do not allow them to originate loans directly from consumers. However, we believe they have developed considerable distribution power through arming brokers with their technology and through strategic alliances with major prime lenders." Kenneth A. Posner, Athina L. Meehan, and Michael D. Courtian, "Specialty Finance: Assessing Impact of Agency Technology on AFS, HI," Morgan Stanley Dean Witter, July 13, 1999, p. 3.

17. As of this writing, such joint ventures include OpenClose.com, LION (Lenders Interactive Online Network), IMX Exchange, and FAST-AU-LP on the Internet.

18. Again, as of this writing, these ventures include iQualify.com, Priceline.com, and Online Mortgage Explorer.

19. Franklin D. Raines, chairman and CEO, Fannie Mae, remarks at Consumers Union, Yonkers, New York, December 8, 1999.

20. See, for example, Kathleen Day, "Fear of What Fannie May Do: Lenders Say the Federally Chartered Company Is Out to Steal Their Business," *Washington Post*, August 8, 1999, p. H1.

21. Bernstein Research. 2000. *The GSEs: Hegemony in the Mortgage Market*, p. 11. New York: BR.

22. Congressional Budget Office, *Assessing the Public Costs and Benefits of Fannie Mae and Freddie Mac* (Washington, D.C.: Government Printing Office, May 1996), p. xii.

23. Congressional Budget Office. *Federal Subsidies and the Housing GSEs* (Washington, D.C.: Government Printing Office, May 2001), p. 5.

24. See, for example, U.S. Senate, Committee on Banking, Housing and Urban Affairs, *Federal National Mortgage Association Public Meeting on Conventional Mortgage Forms Sponsored by Federal National Mortgage Association and Federal Home Loan Mortgage Corporation,* document 92-21, 92nd Congress, 1st session, April 5 and 6, 1971.

25. Urban Institute, *A Study of the GSEs' Single Family Underwriting Guidelines: Final Report,* prepared for the U.S. Department of Housing and Urban Development (Washington, D.C.: UI, April 1999), p. 2.

26. Senator Thomas J. Walsh, "Federal Farm Loan Act: An Address," Senate document 524, 64th Congress, 1st session, August 5, 1916, p. 7.

27. A good historical overview of the FCS is provided by W. Gifford Hoag, *The Farm Credit System: A History of Financial Self-Help* (Danville, Ill.: Interstate Printers & Publishers, 1976).

28. Representative Robert Luce, statement, U.S. House of Representatives, Committee on Banking and Currency, hearings, *Creation of a System of Federal Home Loan Banks,* 72nd Congress, 1st session, March 16, 1932, pp. 12–17, and William E. Best, president, U.S. Building and Loan League, statement, ibid., pp. 28–29. See also John Sprunt Hill, testimony, U.S. Senate, Committee on Banking and Currency, hearings, *Creation of a System of Federal Home Loan Banks,* 72nd Congress, 1st session, January 14, 1932, p. 42.

29. General Accounting Office, *Farmer Mac: Revised Charter Enhances Secondary Market Activity, but Growth Depends on Various Factors,* GAO/GGD-99-85 (Washington, D.C.: GAO, May 1999).

30. Peter J. Wallison, "Leveraging Uncle Sam," *International Economy,* March–April 2000, pp. 32–33 and 59, at p. 59.

31. John C. Weicher, "Housing Finance Fiefdoms: The Privileged Position of Fannie Mae & Freddie Mac," *The American Enterprise,* September–October 1994, pp. 62–67, at p. 62.

32. As Dwight Jaffee has pointed out, the GSE differs from the mercantilist institution in one important respect: the sovereign demanded and received payment in return for issuing a mercantilist charter; by contrast the U.S. government provides the GSEs with additional subsidies and even declines to tax some GSEs to the extent that it taxes other companies. Jaffee, "The Effect on the Mortgage Markets of Privatizing Fannie Mae and Freddie Mac," paper presented at the American Enterprise Institute, May 23, 2000.

Chapter 2: Instrumentalities of Government

1. *Weir v. United States,* 92 F.2d 634 (7th cir., 1937); *United States v. Nowak,* 448 F.2d 134 (7th cir., 1971).

2. *Westfall v. United States*, 274 U.S. 256, 47 S.Ct. 629 (1927).

3. See, for example, Harold Orlans, ed., *Nonprofit Organizations: A Government Management Tool* (New York: Praeger, 1980); Elizabeth T. Boris and C. Eugene Steuerle, *Nonprofits & Government* (Washington, D.C.: Urban Institute Press, 1999); and Paul W. Bonapfel, "The Nature of Public Purpose Authorities: Governmental, Private or Neither?" *Georgia Law Review* 8 (1974): 680–710.

4. *Osborn v. Bank of the United States*, 22 U.S. (9 Wheat.), 738, at 860 (1824).

5. See *T I Federal Credit Union v. Delbonis*, 72 F.3d 921, at 931 (1st cir., 1995).

6. Opinion of the Comptroller General of the United States, B-219801, October 10, 1986.

7. *Department of Employment v. United States*, 385 U.S. 355, 87 S.Ct. 464 (1966) (The American National Red Cross is an instrumentality of the United States and is immune from state taxation).

8. See generally Ronald C. Moe, *Congressionally Chartered Corporate Organizations ("Title 36 Corporations"): What They Are and How Congress Treats Them* (Washington, D.C.: Congressional Research Service, 1999).

9. Attorney General of the United States, "Memorandum re Constitutionality of Senate Confirmation of Persons Nominated by the President as Incorporators and Directors of the Communications Satellite Corp.," reprinted in *Congressional Record*, April 24, 1963, pp. 6977–78 ; letter from Assistant Attorney General William H. Rehnquist to HUD Undersecretary Richard C. Van Dusen, July 10, 1970, concerning status of Fannie Mae directors under federal conflict-of-interest statute.

10. *Lewis v. United States*, 680 F.2d 1239 (9th cir., 1982).

11. See generally Ronald C. Moe, *General Management Laws: A Selective Compendium* (Washington, D.C.: Congressional Research Service, 1999), for an excellent compilation of such laws.

12. Harold Seidman, *Politics, Position, and Power*, 5th ed. (New York,: Oxford University Press, 1998), chap. 10, pp. 161–96, analyzes the distinctions among types of federal agency, including departments and corporations.

13. The act is codified at 31 U.S.C. chap. 91.

14. The 1967 President's Commission on Budget Concepts recommended a unified federal budget that again would have accounted for Fannie Mae's mortgage purchases as federal expenditures. The recommendation necessitated the transition of the corporation to completely private ownership. See *Report of the President's Commission on Budget Concepts* (Washington, D.C.: Government Printing Office, 1967), pp. 29–30.

15. 255 U.S. 180, 41 S.Ct. 243 (1921).

16. One remarkable anomaly is contained in regulations of the Federal Reserve Board, "Obligations eligible as collateral for advances," 12 CFR 201.108, that purports to include GSE obligations as eligible under a statute,

12 U.S.C. sec. 347c, which limits eligibility to obligations of "any agency of the United States."

17. *Mercantile National Bank v. City of New York*, 121 U.S. 138, 154, 7 S.Ct. 826,834 (1887).

18. 12 U.S.C. sec. 1464(a).

19. 12 U.S.C. sec. 1752(i). See also *T I Federal Credit Union v. Delbonis*.

20. General Accounting Office, *Government-Sponsored Enterprises: The Government's Exposure to Risks*, GAO/GGD-90-97 (Washington, D.C.: GAO, 1990), p. 16.

21. 17 U.S. (4 Wheat.) 316 (1819).

22. See, for example, *Doherty v. United States*, 94 F.2d 495 (8th cir., 1938); *United States v. Brown*, 384 F.Supp. 1151 (ED Mich., 1974).

23. General Accounting Office, *Federal Housing Enterprises: HUD's Mission Oversight Needs to Be Strengthened*, GAO/GGD 98-173 (Washington, D.C.: GAO, 1998).

24. June O'Neill, statement, U.S. House of Representatives, Subcommittee on Capital Markets, Securities and Government-Sponsored Enterprises, hearings, *Oversight of the Federal National Mortgage Association [Fannie Mae] and the Federal Home Loan Mortgage Corporation [Freddie Mac]*, 104th Congress, 2nd session, June 12, 1996, pp. 90–91.

25. Variations are possible among GSEs. Until Congress amended Freddie Mac's charter in 1989, it benefited statutorily from sovereign immunity as if it were a government agency. See also *Mendrala v. Crown Mortgage Company*, 955 F.2d 1132 (7th Cir., 1992).

26. See, for example, *Northrip v. Federal National Mortgage Association*, 527 F.2d 23 (6th cir., 1975), holding that the exercise of a private right of sale provision by Fannie Mae was not government action and thus was not subject to the restrictions of the Due Process Clause of the Fifth Amendment.

27. However, the Federal Home Loan Banks are subject to special levies to pay for part of the cost of the savings and loan debacle (the so-called Resolution Funding Corporation, or REFCORP, assessment) and also to contribute to the affordable housing fund.

28. Robert Van Order, "The Economics of Fannie Mae and Freddie Mac," chap. 3 in *Serving Two Masters, Yet Out of Control*, edited by Peter J. Wallison (Washington, D.C.: AEI Press, 2001).

29. See, for example, *Rust v. Johnson*, 597 F.2d 174 (9th cir., 1979), holding that a city's foreclosure of property without taking account of the interests of Fannie Mae as an instrumentality of the federal government amounted to an unconstitutional exercise of state power in violation of the Supremacy Clause. Compare *Federal National Mortgage Association v. Lefkowitz*, 390 F.Supp. 1364 (S.D.N.Y., 1975).

30. The comparison must be understood as only approximate because of

the significant underwriting functions and other activities that the GSEs perform. By contrast Ginnie Mae relies largely on underwriting by the Federal Housing Administration, Department of Veterans Affairs, and Rural Housing Service, whose loans are securitized into Ginnie Mae pools. Also, unlike the GSEs, Ginnie Mae has a single function: the government agency securitizes pools of mortgages that are issued by others. By contrast the GSEs issue securities and also maintain large mortgage portfolios that must be managed.

31. Note, "Personal Liability of Directors of Federal Government Corporations," *Case Western Reserve Law Review* 30 (summer 1980): 733–79.

32. Note, "FNMA and the Rights of Private Investors: Her Heart Still Belongs to Daddy," *Georgetown Law Journal* 59 (November 1970): 369–92.

33. U.S. Senate, Committee on Labor and Human Resources, Subcommittee on Education, Arts and Humanities, *Oversight of Student Loan Marketing Association (Sallie Mae)*, August 12, 1982, p. 135.

34. Oakley Hunter, "The Federal National Mortgage Association: Its Response to Critical Financing Requirements of Housing," *George Washington Law Review* 39: 818–34 (1971), at p. 831; R. S. Seiler Jr.. "Fannie Mae and Freddie Mac as Investor-Owned Utilities, " *Journal of Public Budgeting, Accounting & Financial Management* 11 (1) (spring 1999): 117–54.

35. Sallie Mae, *Annual Report 1973* (Washington, D.C.: Student Loan Marketing Association, 1974).

36. For an extreme case, see Nicholas Lardy, *China's Unfinished Economic Revolution* (Washington, D.C.: Brookings Institution, 1998).

37. See Thomas H. Stanton, "Laws, Cases, and Other Legal Sources on Government-Sponsored Enterprises," ap. A, *A State of Risk* (New York: HarperCollins, 1991), at pp. 206–7; accord, *T I Federal Credit Union v. Delbonis*).

38. Department of Housing and Urban Development, *1987 Report to Congress on the Federal National Mortgage Association* (Washington, D.C.: September 27, 1989), pp. 28–29.

39. Farm Credit System Assistance Board, *The Farm Credit System Assistance Board From Beginning to End: 1992 Annual Report* (Washington, D.C.: December 1, 1992); see generally Kenneth L. Peoples, David Freshwater, Gregory D. Hanson, Paul T. Prentice, and Eric P. Thor, *Anatomy of an American Agricultural Credit Crisis: Farm Debt in the 1980s* (Lanham, Md.: Rowman & Littlefield, 1992).

Chapter 3: Government Support of GSEs

1. Similar listings are presented in Department of the Treasury, *Report of the Secretary of the Treasury on Government Sponsored Enterprises* (Washington, D.C.: Government Printing Office, 1990), p. 4; and Congressional Budget

Office, *Controlling the Risks of Government-Sponsored Enterprises* (Washington, D.C.: Government Printing Office, 1991), p. 8. Legal elements of the implicit federal guarantee are discussed in Thomas H. Stanton, "Laws, Cases, and Other Legal Sources on Government Sponsored Enterprises," ap. A, *A State of Risk* (New York: HarperCollins, 1991), p. 204.

2. For an overview of the early agency credit market, see W. Gifford Hoag, *The Farm Credit System: A History of Financial Self-Help* (Danville, Ill.: Interstate, 1976), pp. 33–44.

3. "The [three federal] Agencies support legislation removing the exemptions from the federal securities laws for equity and unsecured debt securities of Government-sponsored enterprises ('GSEs'), which would require GSEs to register such securities with the SEC." Department of the Treasury, Securities and Exchange Commission, and Board of Governors of the Federal Reserve System, *Joint Report on the Government Securities Market* (Washington, D. C.: Government Printing Office, 1992), p. xvi.

4. 12 U.S.C. sec. 1719(b).

5. Anthony F. Marra, senior vice president and deputy general counsel, Fannie Mae, submission to the Office of the Comptroller of the Currency, Docket 97-22, *Risk-Based Capital Standards: Recourse and Direct Credit Substitutes,* February 3, 1998, p. 4.

6. Dena Aubin, "Fannie Mae Says Gensler Destabilizes Agency Market," Dow Jones Newswires, March 30, 2000.

7. "Fannie Mae Aide Apologizes for Thursday's Statement on Treasury," Dow Jones Newswires, March 30, 2000.

8. See, for example, Robert E. Litan and Jonathan Rauch, *American Finance for the Twenty-first Century* (Washington, D.C.: Brookings Institution, 1998), chap. 4.

9. Congressional Budget Office, *Federal Subsidies and the Housing GSEs* (Washington, D.C.: Government Printing Office, 2001), p. 2

10. One interesting issue relates to political risk: the spreads of benchmark GSE obligations over Treasuries increased significantly in early 2000 after chairman Richard Baker of the House GSE subcommittee and the Treasury each suggested that reducing GSE ties to the federal government might be beneficial.

11. Congressional Budget Office, *The Public Costs and Public Benefits of Fannie Mae and Freddie Mac* (Washington, D.C.: Government Printing Office, 1996), pp. 12–14.

12. The problems of Fannie Mae and the FCS in the 1980s are analyzed in Thomas H. Stanton, "Federal Supervision of Safety and Soundness of Government-Sponsored Enterprises," *Administrative Law Journal* 5 (2) (summer 1991): 395–484.

13. General Accounting Office, *Federal Home Loan Mortgage Corporation: Abuses in Multifamily Program Increase Exposure to Financial Losses*, GAO/RCED-92-6 (Washington, D.C.: GAO, 1991).

14. The FCA reports are quoted in Stanton, "Federal Supervision of Safety and Soundness," at p. 482.

15. Ibid., at pp. 432–33.

16. "Farm Credit System's 'AAA' Eligibility Monitored," *Standard & Poor's Credit Week*, July 20, 1987, p. 13.

17. Department of Housing and Urban Development, *1986 Report to Congress on the Federal National Mortgage Association* (Washington, D.C.: HUD, 1987), p. 100, table V-3.

18. Alan Greenspan, chairman, Federal Reserve Board, "The Role of Capital in Optimal Banking Supervision and Regulation," remarks before the Conference on Capital Regulation in the Twenty-first Century, Federal Reserve Bank of New York, February 26, 1998.

19. The nature of federal supervision of banks and thrift institutions is described in Richard Scott Carnell, "Federal Deposit Insurance and Federal Sponsorship of Fannie Mae and Freddie Mac," chap. 4 in *Serving Two Masters, Yet Out of Control*, edited by Peter J. Wallison (Washington, D.C.: AEI Press, 2001), and Stanton, "Federal Supervision of Safety and Soundness of Government-Sponsored Enterprises," pp. 395–484.

20. See, for example, Kenneth H. Bacon, "Privileged Position: Fannie Mae Expected to Escape Attempt at Tighter Regulation," *Wall Street Journal*, June 19, 1992, p. A1, and Stephen Labaton, "Power of the Mortgage Twins: Fannie and Freddie Guard Autonomy," *New York Times*, November 12, 1991, p. D1.

21. The Government Sponsored Enterprises Financial Safety and Soundness Act of 1991, S. 1282 (introduced by request), reproduced in the *Congressional Record*, June 12, 1991, pp. S7637–S7661 (daily ed.).

22. The Federal Enterprise Regulatory Act of 1991, S. 1621 (introduced by Senator Herbert Kohl for himself and for Senators John Glenn and Carl Levin).

23. Budget restrictions can seriously impede a regulator. The Office of Secondary Market Oversight, an independent part of the FCA that supervises Farmer Mac, has been so constrained by budget controls—added at the GSE's behest—that it could not afford to hire a secretary for the director of the office.

24. See, for example, 12 U.S.C. sec. 1818 and 3907.

25. Some years ago James Pierce made this point about the process of bank examination:

Government supervisors who interrogate bankers earn maybe sixty thousand dollars a year; the people they question often make ten or twenty times that and operate out of offices that make a regulator's quarters look like a shelter for the homeless. How can regulators second-guess the management of these multinational corporations [?] ... The answer is clear: regulators cannot substitute their judgment for a bank manager's, even at a small bank, where dealings are generally easier to track.

James L. Pierce, *The Future of Banking* (New Haven: Yale University Press, 1991), pp. 99–100.

26. Thomas H. Stanton, "Pending Legislation Would End Impasse over SBA Legislation: Congress May Create a New Corporation to Aid Small Business but Has Drafted the Law in a Way That May Ultimately Expose the Government to Significant Financial Losses," *Legal Times*, October 6, 1986, pp. 24–26.

27. Treasury Department, *1991 Report of the Secretary of the Treasury on Government-Sponsored Enterprises* (Washington, D.C.: Government Printing Office, 1991), p. 8

28. See Charles Bowsher, Comptroller General of the United States, testimony, U.S. Senate, Committee on Governmental Affairs, Subcommittee on Government Information and Regulation, "Various Proposals to Regulate GSE's and to Examine the Risk These Entities Pose to U.S. Taxpayers," S. Hrg 102-621, 102nd Congress, 1st session, July 18, 1991, pp. 2–8, and the Federal Enterprise Regulatory Act of 1991, S. 1621 (introduced by Senator Herbert Kohl for himself and for Senators John Glenn and Carl Levin).

29. 12 U.S. Code sec. 2277a.

30. See, for example, U.S. House of Representatives, Committee on the Budget, *Omnibus Budget Reconciliation Act of 1990*, report to accompany H.R. 5835, October 16, 1990; and *Congressional Record*, October 16, 1990, p. H 10332 (colloquy between Rep. J. J. Pickle and Rep. Leon Panetta).

31. Enacted legislation includes the safety and soundness parts of (1) the Federal Housing Enterprises Financial Safety and Soundness Act of 1992, Pub. L. 102-550; (2) the Farm Credit Banks and Associations Safety and Soundness Act of 1992, Pub. L. No. 102-552; and (3) the Higher Education Act of 1992, Pub. L. 102-325.

32. See *Revenue Act of 1992*, conference report to accompany H.R. 11, House Report 102-1034, title 13, "Federal Debt Management Responsibility," 102nd Congress, 2nd session, October 5, 1992, pp. 669–671.

33. For the perspective of the investment bankers who bought up obligations of the failed FCS in 1987 and who scorned the people who unloaded their FCS obligations at a discount, see Michael Lewis, *Liar's Poker* (New York: W. W. Norton, 1989), p. 175.

34. Harold Seidman, "The Quasi World of the Federal Government," *Brookings Review*, summer 1988, pp. 23–27, at p. 25.

35. First, reform has frequently been crisis-oriented. Despite an awareness of the structural defects in the financial system or in the monetary authority, little effort is directed toward reform until a crisis has occurred or is about to occur. . . . Second, related to the crisis-orientation of reform, financial reform is frequently myopic and backward-looking. It is designed to deal in *ad hoc* fashion with an immediate set of problems usually within a specific sector of the financial system.

Thomas F. Cargill and Gillian G. Garcia, *Financial Reform of the 1980s* (Stanford: Hoover Institution Press, 1985), p. 38.

36. To borrow the felicitous words of William McChesney Martin from another context, the regulator may be required to take away the punch bowl just when the party gets going.

37. The problem occurred when the FCS failed in the mid-1980s. As discussed in chapter 5, many powerful members of Congress persisted in protecting the cooperative FCS shareholders from the financial consequences of the failure.

38. Compare Dena Aubin, "Fannie Mae Says Gensler Destabilizes Agency Market," Dow Jones Newswires, March 30, 2000, and "Fannie Mae Aide Apologizes for Thursday's Statement on Treasury," Dow Jones Newswires, March 30, 2000, with Albert B. Crenshaw, "CBO Faults Subsidies for 2 Finance Firms," *Washington Post*, May 30, 1996, p. D9, and Richard W. Stevenson, "Report Is Skeptical of U.S.-Backed Home Mortgages," *New York Times*, May 30, 1996, p. D1.

39. General Accounting Office, *Federal Housing Enterprises: HUD's Mission Oversight Needs to be Strengthened*, GAO/GGD-98-173 (Washington, D.C.: GAO, 1998), p. 12.

40. On the latter point, see "Risk-Based Capital White Paper," transmitted by Jamie S. Gorelick, vice-chairman, Fannie Mae, to Jacob Lew, director, Office of Management and Budget, March 3, 1999, at p. 1: "The approach OFHEO appears to have taken . . . can drive up the cost of mortgage finance for all home buyers. But its effect will be greatest on the low-income, minority and other special needs borrowers we serve."

Chapter 4: The Public Purposes of GSEs

1. Compare the opinion of Justice Brandeis in *Texas Pac. Ry. Co. v. Pottorf*: "National banks lack power to pledge their assets to secure private deposits. The measure of their powers is the statutory grant; and powers not conferred by Congress are denied. For the act under which national banks are organized constitutes a complete system for their government." 291 U.S. 245 at 253, 54 S.Ct. 416 at 417 (1934).

2. 12 U.S.C. sec. 1717 (b)(2).

3. *Texas Pac. Ry. Co. v. Pottorf.*

4. Fannie Mae charter act, 12 U.S.C. sec. 1723 (a).

5. National banks are limited to express powers plus "all such incidental powers as shall be necessary to carry on the business of banking." 12 U.S.C. sec. 24.

6. 20 U.S.C. sec. 1087-2 (d)(1)(E).

7. See, for example, *First American Federal Savings and Loan Association et al. v. Student Loan Marketing Association*, 84-1014 CIV-5 (E.D.N.C., 1985, unpublished opinion), and *Fidelity Financial Corp. v. Federal Home Loan Bank of San Francisco*, 589 F.Supp. 885 (1983), *aff'd* 792 F.2d 1432 (9th cir., 1986).

8. But see *Bowling v. Block*, 785 F2d 556, affirming a lower court decision at 602 F. Supp. 667, holding that FCS borrowers and other private parties lacked standing both under the Farm Credit Act and under the Administrative Procedure Act.

9. *Association of Data Processing Service Organizations v. Federal Home Loan Bank Board*, 568 F.2d 478 (6th Cir., 1977); and *Central Bank, N.A. v. Federal Home Loan Bank of San Francisco*, 430 F.Supp. 1080 (N.D. Calif., 1977), vacated and remanded, 620 F.2d 309 (9th cir., 1980).

10. 472 F.2d 427 (1st cir., 1972).

11. Compare *Independent Insurance Agents of America, Inc. v. Hawke*, F.3rd (D.C. cir., 2000).

12. See generally Richard Bartke, "Fannie Mae and the Secondary Mortgage Market," *Northwestern University Law Review* 66 (March–April 1971): 833–64.

13. P.L. 91-351. See generally Richard Bartke, "Home Financing at the Crossroads—A Study of the Federal Home Loan Mortgage Corporation," *Indiana Law Journal* 48 (fall 1972): 1–42.

14. See, for example, U.S. and English cases cited in Edwin Merrick Dodd, *American Business Corporations until 1860* (Cambridge: Harvard University Press, 1954), pp. 104–09.

15. *REW Enterprises, Inc. v. Premier Bank, N.A.*, 49 F.3d 163 (5th cir., 1995).

16. 49 F.3d at 171.

17. Department of Housing and Urban Development, "Regulations Governing Operations of the Federal National Mortgage Association, Common Stock," *Federal Register* 36 (60) (March 27, 1971): 5784–5 (amending 24 CFR sec. 81.2).

18. *Texas Savings & Community Bankers Assn. v. Federal Housing Finance Board*, 98-50758, F.3d (5th cir., 2000), decided January 20, 2000.

19. 467 U.S. 837, 104 S.Ct. 2778 (1984); see also *NationsBank of N.C. v. Variable Annuity Life Ins.*, 513 U.S. 251 (1995).

20. But see *Christensen v. Harris County*, U.S. (May 1, 2000) (courts will accord *Chevron* deference to an agency's regulation, but not to an opinion letter not based on a regulation).

21. See, for example, *Independent Bankers Ass'n v. Farm Credit Admin*, 986 F. Supp. 663 (D.D.C., 1997).

22. The pattern has also been true for banking regulators that have sought to expand the powers of the institutions that they oversee. See, for example, Jeffrey D. Dunn, "Expansion of National Bank Powers: Regulatory and Judicial Precedent under the National Bank Act, Glass-Steagall Act, and Bank Holding Company Act," *Southwestern Law Journal* 36 (2) (June 1982): 765–92, and more recently *NationsBank of N.C. v. Variable Annuity Life Ins.*, 513 U.S. 251 (1995).

23. 20 U.S.C. sec. 1087-2(h)(2). The provision illustrates a common ambiguity in GSE charter acts: a provision hidden in a subparagraph purports to affect an entire "section" of law.

24. 12 U.S.C. sec. 4542(a).

25. 12 U.S.C. sec. 4541.

26. See, for example, *National Petroleum Refiners Association v. Federal Trade Commission*, 482 F.2d 672 (D.C. cir., 1973); *Independent Bankers Ass'n v. Heimann*, 613 F2d 1164, 1169 (D.C. cir., 1979), *cert. den.* 449 U.S. 823, 101 S.Ct. 84 (1980); and *Lincoln Savings and Loan Ass'n v. Federal Home Loan Bank Board*, 856 F.2d 1558 (D.C. cir., 1988).

27. Carla A. Hills, secretary of housing and urban development, letter to Senator William Proxmire, December 9, 1976; reprinted in U.S. Senate, Committee on Banking, Housing and Urban Affairs, "Secondary Market Operations of the Federal National Mortgage Association and the Federal Home Loan Mortgage Corporation," hearings, 94th Congress, 2nd session, December 1976, pp. 627–35.

28. Robert S. Seiler Jr., "Fannie Mae and Freddie Mac as Investor-Owned Utilities," *Journal of Public Budgeting, Accounting & Financial Management* 11 (1) (spring 1999): 134–44.

29. Robert Julavits, "HUD Presses Fannie Mae and Freddie Mac to Defend New Businesses," *American Banker*, January 6, 2000; William C. Apgar, assistant secretary for housing and federal housing commissioner, letter from to Jamie Gorelick, vice-chairman, Fannie Mae, December 21, 1999; and Apgar, letter from to David W. Glenn, president, Freddie Mac, December 21, 1999.

30. Boston Consulting Group, *The Information Superhighway and Retail Banking* (Boston: Bank Administration Institute, 1995).

31. Lowell L. Bryan, *Bankrupt: Restoring the Health and Profitability of Our Banking System* (New York: HarperCollins, 1991).

32. *NationsBank of N.C. v. Variable Annuity Life Ins.*, 513 U.S. 251 (1995).

33. Andrew M. Cuomo, secretary of housing and urban development, letter to James A. Johnson, chairman and chief executive officer, Fannie Mae, June 23, 1997.

34. Freddie Mac spokesperson, quoted in *Inside Mortgage Finance*, "Regional Banks Butt Heads with Freddie Mac over GSE Interest in HomeAdvisor Technologies," May 5, 2000.

35. 12 U.S.C. sec. 1717 (b)(2) (Fannie Mae Charter Act); see also 12 U.S.C. sec. 1454 (a)(2) (Freddie Mac Charter Act).

36. 12 U.S.C. sec. 1716 (a) (Fannie Mae Charter Act); see also 12 U.S.C. note to sec. 1451 (Freddie Mac Charter Act).

37. One such effort related to HUD's review of Fannie Mae's intent to issue the new multiclass form of mortgage-backed security known as a REMIC (real estate mortgage investment conduit). See, for example, Michael McQueen and Ann Monroe, "Debate on New U.S.-Backed Mortgage Security Stirs Charges of Greed, Government Domination,"*Wall Street Journal*, April 20, 1987, p. 48.

38. John Connor, "Freddie Mac May Get Authority to Buy Riskier Down-Payment Mortgages," *Wall Street Journal*, October 7, 1998, p. B2.

39. James Dao, "D'Amato's Mortgage Measure Faces a Repeal by Congress; His Plan Favored a Campaign Contributor," *New York Times*, October 20, 1998, p. A28.

40. Congressman Richard Baker, "H.R.1409—Secondary Mortgage Market Enterprises Regulatory Improvement Act—Section-by-Section Summary," April 5, 2001.

Chapter 5: Origins of the Legal Framework of GSEs

1. Del. Code Ann. tit. 8, sec. 121(a).

2. Samuel Williston, "History of the Law of Business Corporations before 1800," *Harvard Law Review* 2 (3, 4) (October–November 1888).

3. The growth of the joint-stock corporation eventually permitted the creation of corporations with a longer-term financial base. See Williston, "History of the Law," pp. 109–110, and generally William Robert Scott, *The Constitution and Finance of English, Scottish and Irish Joint-Stock Companies to 1720s* (Cambridge: Cambridge University Press, 1912; reprinted Gloucester, Mass.: Peter Smith, 1968).

4. Adam Smith, *The Wealth of Nations*, bk. 5, chap. 1, pt. 3 (New York: Random House, 1937), p. 691. Smith did look more favorably on the use of special-purpose charters in banking.

5. On the reluctance of the United States to build a centralized administrative state, see Richard J. Stillman 2, *Preface to Public Administration: A Search for Themes and Direction*, 2nd ed. (Burke, Va.: Chatelaine Press, 1998).

6. Leverett S. Lyon, Myron W. Watkins, and Victor Abramson, *Government and Economic Life: Development and Current Issues of American Public Policy*, vol. 1 (Washington, D.C.: Brookings Institution, 1939), p. 51–55; *Louis K. Liggett Co. v. Lee*, 233 U.S. 517 at 541 (1933) (dissent of Justice Brandeis).

7. Joseph S. Davis, *Essays in the Earlier History of American Corporations* (Cambridge: Harvard University Press, 1917), pp. 36–44; Bray Hammond, *Banks and Politics in America from the Revolution to the Civil War* (Princeton: Princeton University Press, 1957), 52ff.

8. Alexander Hamilton, *Report on a National Bank* (December 14, 1790), reprinted in *Papers on Public Credit, Commerce, and Finance*, edited by Samuel McKee Jr. (New York: Columbia University Press, 1934), p. 76.

9. Davis, *Essays in the Earlier History*, pp. 100–101.

10. See "An Act to Incorporate the Subscribers to the Bank of the United States," approved February 25, 1791, 1 Statutes-at-Large, 191.

11. *McCulloch v. Maryland*, 17 U.S. (4 Wheat.) 316 (1819), and *Osborn v. Bank of the United States*, 22 U.S. (9 Wheat.) 738 (1824).

For national banks, see, for example, *First Nat'l Bank v. Missouri*, 263 U.S. 640 (1924); *First Nat'l Bank v. Fellows*, 244 U.S. 416 (1917); *Easton v. Iowa*, 188 U.S. 220 (1903); and *Davis v. Elmira Sav. Bank*, 161 U.S. 275 (1896).

For government-sponsored enterprises, see, for example, *Smith v. Kansas City Title & Trust Company, et al.*, 255 U.S. 180 (1920); *Federal Land Bank v. Bismarck Lumber Co.*, 314 U.S. 95 (1941); *Federal Land Bank v. Priddy*, 29 U. S. 229 (1935); *Fahey v. O'Melveny & Meyers*, 200 F.2d 420 (9th Cir., 1952); *Ass'n of Data Processing, Inc. v. Federal Home Loan Bank*, 568 F.2d 478 (6th Cir., 1977); *Northrip v. Federal Nat'l Mortgage Ass'n*, 527 F.2d 23 (6th Cir., 1975); and *Rust v. Johnson*, 597 F.2d 174 (9th Cir., 1979).

12. Hammond, *Banks and Politics in America*, p. 424; Albert S. Bolles, *The Financial History of the United States From 1789 to 1860* (New York: D. Appleton, 1883), pp. 339–42.

13. National Academy of Public Administration, *Report on Government Corporations* (Washington, D.C.: NAPA, 1981), p. 32, and Herman Schwartz, "Governmentally Appointed Directors in a Private Corporation: The Communications Satellite Act of 1962," *Harvard Law Review* 79 (1965): 350–64.

The logic for the use of government-appointed directors for government-sponsored enterprises relates to the government's goal of promoting the distribution of benefits to constituencies intended to be served by the enterprise. Nevertheless, because of factors including the fiduciary obligations of directors to the company and its shareholders, public directors add little more federal control than would be available from any other members of the board of directors of an enterprise. See Thomas H. Stanton, *A State of Risk* (New York: HarperCollins, 1991), pp. 207–8.

14. The history of this unusual structure is recounted in Marriner S.

Eccles, *Beckoning Frontiers: Public and Personal Recollections* (New York: Knopf, 1951).

15. See, for example, *Melcher v. Federal Open Market Committee*, 644 F.Supp. 510 (D.D.C., 1986).

16. See Thomas H. Stanton, testimony, U.S. House of Representatives, Committee on Banking and Financial Services, Subcommittee on Capital Markets, Securities, and Government-Sponsored Enterprises, "Oversight Hearing on the Federal Home Loan Bank System," 104th Congress, 1st session, September 28, 1995, pp. 247–49.

17. See, for example, *Union Pacific Railroad Co. v. United States (Sinking Fund Cases)*, 99 S.Ct. 700 (1878), holding that Congress retained the authority to amend, alter, or repeal the charter of the Union Pacific Railroad Company.

18. *Colorado Springs Production Credit Association v. Farm Credit Administration*, 967 F.2d 648 (D.C. Cir., 1992).

19. *Fahey v. O'Melveny & Myers*, 200 F.2d 420, 446 (9th Cir., 1952).

20. 12 U.S.C. sec. 1717(a)(2)(B).

21. Fritz Redlich, *The Molding of American Banking: Men and Ideas*, pt. 1 (New York: Hafner Publishing, 1947), pp. 151, 152, 154.

22. U.S. Railway Commission, *Report of the U.S. Pacific Railway Commission* (Washington, D.C.: Government Printing Office, 1887), p. 121.

23. Harold Seidman, *Politics, Position, and Power*, 5th ed. (New York: Oxford University Press, 1998), p. 23. For the FCS perspective, see W. N. Stokes Jr., "Independence and More Member Control," chap. 5, *Credit to Farmers* (Washington, D.C.: Federal Intermediate Credit Banks, 1973), pp. 99–114. The 1953 legislation marked the return of the FCS to independent financial and institutional status after its government rescue in the aftermath of the Great Depression.

24. Harold Seidman, testimony (relating to the application of the Government Corporation Control Act to the FCS), U.S. House of Representatives, Committee on Government Operations, Subcommittee on Executive and Legislative Reorganization, *Amending the Government Corporation Control Act*, subcommittee hearing, February 1958.

25. See, for example, Albert R. Karr, "Farm Credit System, under Orders to Get Tough, Is Hampered by Lawmaker Pleas for Leniency," *Wall Street Journal*, May 29, 1986, p. 34.

26. U.S. House of Representatives, Committee on Banking, Finance and Urban Affairs, *Report*, document 102-206, 102nd Congress, 1st session, September 17, 1991, p. 115 (dissenting view of Rep. Jim Leach).

27. "Shaping Up Fannie Mae and Freddie Mac: Uncle Sam Sends Them Next Door," *Economist*, May 19, 1990, p. 92; Carol Matlack, "Getting Their Way," *National Journal*, October 27, 1990, pp. 2584–88.

28. Department of the Treasury, *Government Sponsorship of the Federal National Mortgage Association and the Federal Home Loan Mortgage Corporation* (Washington, D.C.: Government Printing Office, 1996), p. 81.

29. See, for example, Jackie Calmes, "Federal Mortgage Firm Is Facing New Assault to Privileged Status: But Fannie Has Clout to Counter the Agencies That Seek to Privatize It," *Wall Street Journal*, May 14, 1986, p. 1; Chairman Richard Baker, comments, U.S. House of Representatives, Committee on Banking and Financial Services, Subcommittee on Capital Markets, Securities, and Government-Sponsored Enterprises, "Oversight of the Federal National Mortgage Association [Fannie Mae] and the Federal Home Loan Mortgage Corporation [Freddie Mac]," 104th Congress, 2nd session, July 24, 1996, pp. 136–41.

30. The figures come from "Fannie, Freddie Lobbying Spending Jumps Significantly in 1999, Latest Filings Reveal," *Inside Mortgage Finance*, December 10, 1999.

31. "Mortgage-Related Groups Spend Record $18 Million in Political Lobbying in 1999," *Inside Mortgage Finance*, June 30, 2000; "Freddie Mac Setting Record in Terms of Soft Money Donations to Political Parties," *Inside MBS & ABS*, August 11, 2000.

32. Many other parts of the GSE charter benefit from active political defense as well. See, for example, John H. Cushman Jr., "Powerful Corporation Persuades House Panel to Retreat on Tax," *New York Times*, June 24, 1993, p. A-18 (Fannie Mae defense of its statutory exemption from the obligation to pay income taxes to the District of Columbia).

33. One notable exception was the Farm Credit System, which did not bet the bank after its financial failure in the mid-1980s. The action may have been a function of the system's intricate cooperative structure, which limited the opportunities for such action.

Chapter 6: The Consequences of Organizational Form and Governance

1. See, for example, *Dodge v. Ford Motor Company*, 204 Mich. 459, 170 N.W. 668 (1919).

2. *Osborn v. Bank of the United States* (although it carries out public purposes as specified by law, the Bank of the United States is a private company created to earn profits for its shareholders); see also William H. Rehnquist, assistant attorney general, Office of Legal Counsel, Department of Justice, letter to Richard C. Van Dusen, under secretary of housing and urban development, July 10, 1970, at p. 3 ("Both general corporate statutes and the common law have traditionally imposed an obligation of fidelity and fair dealing

on directors of non-governmental corporations, and the directors of FNMA are undoubtedly subject to such obligations.").

3. *Dodge v. Ford Motor Co.,* 204 Mich. 459, 170 N.W. 668 (1919). Compare *A.P. Smith Mfg. Co. v. Barlow*, 13 N.J. 145, 92 A2d 581 (1953).

4. Quoted in Stephen Taub and Jackey Gold, "Twilight Zone,"*Financial World*, December 12, 1989, p. 46.

5. See note, "Personal Liability of Directors of Federal Government Corporations," *Case Western Reserve Law Review*, 1980, pp. 733–79.

6. Carla A. Hills, secretary of housing and urban development, letter to Senator William Proxmire, December 9, 1976; reprinted in U. S. Senate, Committee on Banking, Housing and Urban Affairs, "Secondary Market Operations of the Federal National Mortgage Association and the Federal Home Loan Mortgage Corporation," hearings, 94th Congress, 2nd session, December 1976, pp. 627–35, at p. 628.

7. Farm Credit Administration, *The Director's Role: Farm Credit System Institutions* (McLean, Va.: Farm Credit Administration, 1997), p. 3.

8. 12 CFR pt. 612, "Standards of Conduct."

9. Federal Housing Finance Board, proposed rule, "Powers and Responsibilities of Federal Home Loan Bank Boards of Directors and Senior Management," *Federal Register* 65 (1): 81–91, at 81–82. The rule became final with an effective date of May 31, 2000.

10. See, for example, U.S. Department of the Treasury, *Government Sponsorship of the Federal National Mortgage Association and the Federal Home Loan Mortgage Corporation* (Washington, D.C.: Government Printing Office, 1996), p. 81.

11. Congressional Budget Office, *The Public Costs and Public Benefits of Fannie Mae and Freddie Mac* (Washington, D.C.: 1996), p. 35.

12. Pub. L. 94-200, title 3, Dec. 31, 1975, 89 Stat. 1125, codified at 12 U.S.C. sec. 2801 et seq.

13. William C. Apgar, assistant secretary for housing and federal housing commissioner, statement before the U.S. House of Representatives, Committee on Banking and Financial Services, Subcommittee on Capital Markets, Securities and Government Sponsored Enterprises, March 22, 2000, p. 1 of prepared text.

14. Department of Housing and Urban Development, "HUD's Regulation of the Federal National Mortgage Association (Fannie Mae) and the Federal Home Loan Mortgage Corporation (Freddie Mac); Proposed Rule," *Federal Register* 65 (47) (March 9, 2000): 12631–816, at 12638.

15. General Accounting Office, *Federal Housing Enterprises: HUD's Mission Oversight Needs to Be Strengthened*, GAO/GGD-98-173 (Washington, D.C.: GAO, 1998), p. 59.

16. For similar 1997 and 1998 data, see Department of Housing and Ur-

ban Development, "HUD's Regulation of the Federal National Mortgage Association (Fannie Mae) and the Federal Home Loan Mortgage Corporation (Freddie Mac); Proposed Rules," *Federal Register* 65 (47) (March 9, 2000): 12631–816 at 12688.

17. Barry P. Bosworth, Andrew S. Carron, and Elisabeth H. Rhyne, *The Economics of Federal Credit Programs* (Washington, D.C.: Brookings Institution, 1987), p. 72; see also Office of Federal Housing Enterprise Oversight, *2000 Report to Congress* (Washington, D.C.: 2000), at p. 28.

18. Leland Brendsel, CEO, Freddie Mac, testimony, U.S. House of Representatives, Committee on Ways and Means, Subcommittee on Oversight, *Government-Sponsored Enterprises*, serial 101-65, 101st Congress, 1st session, September 28, 1989, at p. 53.

19. Ibid., at pp. 99–100.

20. See, for example, Kenneth A. Posner, Morgan Stanley Dean Witter, "Freddie Mac (FRE): Fast Growth, Wide Margins, Raising Estimates," *Investment Research*, July 16, 1999, justifying a "strong buy" for Freddie Mac stock on the grounds that, among other developments, "wild portfolio growth continues. Freddie's retained portfolio grew $20 billion in 2Q99, equivalent to a quarterly annualized growth rate of 29 percent, surpassing our $12 billion growth forecast by a healthy margin."

21. A good but dated overview of the legal structure of the Federal Home Loan Bank System is found in Dirk S. Adams, Rodney R. Peck, and Jill W. Spencer, "FIRREA and the New Federal Home Loan Bank System," *Santa Clara Law Review* 32 (1) (1992): 17–60.

22. Richard W. Bartke, "Fannie Mae and the Secondary Mortgage Market," *Northwestern University Law Review* 66 (March–April 1971): 1–78.

23. "Privacy Becomes Fannie Mae," *Business Week*, August 30, 1969, pp. 44–46.

24. Richard W. Bartke, "Home Financing at the Crossroads: A Study of the Federal Home Loan Mortgage Corporation," *Indiana Law Journal* 48 (fall 1972): 1–42.

25. U.S. Senate, Committee on Banking, Housing and Urban Affairs, *Federal National Mortgage Association Public Meeting on Conventional Mortgage Forms*, 92nd Congress, 1st session, April 5 and 6, 1971, Document 92-21 (Washington, D.C.: Government Printing Office, 1971).

26. Ellen P. Roche, "A New Housing Finance Vision: Universal Accounts Could Make Mortgages Obsolete," *Secondary Mortgage Markets*, July 1997, pp. 23–28.

27. Kathleen Day, "Fear of What Fannie May Do: Lenders Say the Federally Chartered Company Is Out to Steal Their Business," *Washington Post*, August 8, 1999, p. H1.

28. For an interesting early example of Fannie Mae's successful defense of its governance structures, see U.S. Senate, Committee on Banking, Housing and Urban Affairs, hearings on S. 1397, 95th Congress, 1st session, June 7–8, 1977.

29. Congressional Budget Office, *Federal Subsidies and the Housing GSEs* (Washington, D.C.: Government Printing Office, 2001), p. 5.

30. Congressional Budget Office, *Assessing the Public Costs and Benefits of Fannie Mae and Freddie Mac* (Washington, D.C.: 1996), p. xiii.

31. Thomas H. Stanton, "Government-Sponsored Enterprises and Changing Markets: The Need for an Exit Strategy," *Financier: Analyses of Capital and Money Market Transactions* 2 (2) (May 1995): 27–42.

32. CBO, *Federal Subsidies and the Housing GSEs*, p. 5.

Chaper 7: Changing Markets and Exit Strategies

1. Office of Management and Budget, "Government Sponsored Enterprises (GSEs)," ap. 1, *Memorandum on Government Corporations*, M-96-05 (Washington, D.C.: Government Printing Office, 1995), pp. 14–15.

2. Congressional Budget Office, *Assessing the Public Costs and Benefits of Fannie Mae and Freddie Mac* (Washington, D.C.: Government Printing Office, 1996), p. xii.

3. Darcy Bradbury, deputy assistant secretary of the Treasury for federal finance, statement, U.S. House of Representatives, Committee on Economic and Educational Opportunities, Subcommittee on Postsecondary Education, Training and Lifelong Learning, and Committee on Government Reform and Oversight, Subcommittee on National Economic Growth, Natural Resources and Regulatory Affairs, May 3, 1995.

4. The memorandum continues:

A GSE could be fully privatized when the:
1. Assigned functions themselves are no longer necessary or appropriate for Federal involvement.
2. Business conditions which prompted its creation have changed (i.e., the special privileges bestowed upon them are no longer necessary to perform the functions for which they were created), or
3. A GSE is no longer the most efficient way to achieve the public purpose.

OMB, "GSEs," pp. 14–15.

5. Sallie Mae, *The Restructuring of Sallie Mae: Rationale and Feasibility* (Washington, D.C.: Student Loan Marketing Association, 1994), pp. 13–14 (emphasis in original).

6. See Thomas H. Stanton, "Efficient and Smaller Government: The Search for an Illusion?" *Ripon Forum* 34 (2) (fall 1999): 23–26.

7. David Stockman, *The Triumph of Politics: How the Reagan Revolution Failed* (New York: Harper & Row, 1986).

8. Lawrence A. Kudlow, Office of Management and Budget, statement, U.S. House of Representatives, Committee on Banking, Finance and Urban Affairs, Subcommittee on Housing and Community Development, *To Expand and Reorganize the Federal Home Loan Mortgage Corporation*, hearings, 97th Congress, 2nd session, June 3, 1982, p. 501.

9. Office of the President, President's Private Sector Survey on Cost Control Task Force on Boards/Commissions-Banking, *Bank 35: Neutralizing Agency Status of FNMA and FHLMC* (Washington, D.C.: 1983), at p. 236 (emphasis in original).

10. Joseph Wright Jr., deputy director, Office of Management and Budget, communication to David O. Maxwell, chairman and CEO, Fannie Mae, March 3, 1986.

11. James A. Baker 3d, letter to Sen. Lowell P. Weicker Jr., chairman, Senate Committee on Small Business, October 1, 1986.

12. David A. Vise, "The Money Machine: How Fannie Mae Wields Power," *Washington Post*, January 16, 1995, p. A14. Many other articles could be cited, for example, John H. Cushman Jr., "Powerful Corporation Persuades House Panel to Retreat on Tax," *New York Times*, June 24, 1993, p. A18.

13. *Assessing the Public Costs and Benefits*, p. 44.

14. Albert B. Crenshaw, "CBO Faults Subsidies for Two Finance Firms," *Washington Post*, May 30, 1996, p. D9; and Richard W. Stevenson, "Report Is Skeptical of U.S.-Backed Home Mortgages," *New York Times*, May 30, 1996, p. D1.

15. The Student Loan Marketing Association Reorganization Act of 1996, tit. 6, Pub. L. 104-208, enacted September 30, 1996.

16. Lawrence A. Hough, president and CEO, Sallie Mae, testimony, U.S. Senate, Committee on Labor and Human Resources, Subcommittee on Education, Arts and Humanities, *Privatization of Sallie Mae and Connie Lee*, hearing, 104th Congress, 1st session, June 20, 1995, p. 12.

17. Codified at 20 U.S.C. sec. 1087-2 (h) (7).

18. *Privatization of Sallie Mae and Connie Lee*, p. 4.

19. Sanford Bernstein & Co., Bernstein Research, "Sallie Mae: Metamorphasis" (New York: SB, 1997), quoted in John E. Dean, Saul L. Moskowitz, and Karen L. Cipriani, "Implications of the Privatization of Sallie Mae," *Journal of Public Budgeting, Accounting & Financial Management* 11 (1) (spring 1999): 56–80, n 35.

20. Dean, Moskowitz, and Cipriani, ibid., p. 62.

21. See the Student Loan Marketing Association Reorganization Act of 1996; Sallie Mae, *Proxy Statement/Prospectus* (Washington, D.C.: Sallie Mae, July 10, 1997), and Dean, Moskowitz, and Cipriani, ibid.

22. The nonaffiliation provisions are found in separate laws, the Federal Deposit Insurance Act, 12 U.S.C. sec. 1828(s) and the Federal Credit Union Act, 12 U.S.C. sec. 1781(e).

23. Dean, Moskowitz, and Cipriani, "Privatization of Sallie Mae," p. 68.

24. Albert B. Crenshaw, "Sallie Mae to Acquire Student-Loan Rival," *Washington Post*, June 16, 2000, p. E1.

25. The 1996 Treasury Department and Congressional Budget Office studies have been cited in the present volume. See also General Accounting Office, *Housing Enterprises: Potential Impacts of Severing Government Sponsorship*, GAO/GGD-96-120 (Washington, D.C.: GAO, 1996); Department of Housing and Urban Development, *Privatization of Fannie Mae and Freddie Mac: Desirability and Feasibility* (Washington, D.C.: HUD, 1996), and *Studies on Privatizing Fannie Mae and Freddie Mac* (Washington, D.C.: HUD, 1996).

26. Ellen P. Roche, "A New Housing Finance Vision: Universal Accounts Could Make Mortgages Obsolete," *Secondary Mortgage Markets*, July 1997, pp. 23–28.

27. Kenneth R. Harney, "New Breed of Mortgage to Carry Built-in Portability," *Washington Post*, January 15, 2000, p. G1.

28. Dean, Moskowitz, and Cipriani, "Privatization of Sallie Mae," p. 67.

29. Office of Management and Budget, *Budget of the United States Government, Fiscal Year 2000: Analytical Perspectives* (Washington, D.C.: Government Printing Office, 1999), p. 114 (tax expenditures), and *Budget of the United States Government, Fiscal Year 2002: Analytical Perspectives* (Washington, D.C.: Government Printing Office, 2001), p. 268 (current services outlays).

30. The policy option is presented in more detail in Thomas H. Stanton, "An Alternative Approach to GSE Reform through National Mortgage Associations," chap. 11, in *Serving Two Masters, Yet Out of Control*, edited by Peter J. Wallison (Washington, D.C.: AEI Press, 2001).

31. William Robert Scott, *The Constitution and Finance of English, Scottish and Irish Joint-Stock Companies to 1720s* (Cambridge: Cambridge University Press, 1912; reprinted Gloucester, Mass.: Peter Smith, 1968). Vol. 1, chap. 6, reports that already in the late sixteenth century the British Parliament became concerned about issues of monopoly in charters.

32. William R. Anson, *The Law and Custom of the Constitution*, vol. 2, *The Crown*, pt. 1, 4th ed. (Oxford: Clarendon Press, 1935), pp. 320–21.

33. Arthur Meier Schlesinger, *The Colonial Merchants and the American Revolution, 1763–1776* (New York: Columbia University, 1918), pp. 279–304.

34. Kathleen Day, "Fear of What Fannie May Do: Lenders Say the Federally Chartered Company Is Out to Steal Their Business," *Washington Post*, August 8, 1999, p. H1.

Index

About the Author

THOMAS H. STANTON is a Washington, D.C., attorney. His practice relates to the capacity of public institutions to deliver services effectively, with specialties relating to organizational design, implementation of federal programs, and regulatory oversight. Mr. Stanton is the chairman of the Standing Panel on Executive Organization and Management of the National Academy of Public Administration and a former member of the Senior Executive Service.

Mr. Stanton has provided legal and policy counsel regarding the design and operation of government programs to federal, state, local, and international organizations and to federal agencies and offices. He is a fellow of the Center for the Study of American Government at the Johns Hopkins University, where he teaches graduate seminars on the law of public institutions, government and the American economy, and government and the credit markets.

The author's writings on government and the financial markets include a book on government-sponsored enterprises, *A State of Risk* (HarperCollins, 1991) and numerous articles. The concerns expressed in that book helped lead to enactment of several pieces of legislation and the creation of a new federal financial regulator in 1992. He has been an invited witness before many congressional committees and subcommittees and recently testified on legislative proposals to create an Office of National Homeland Security.

Mr. Stanton earned his B.A. degree from the University of California at Davis, M.A. from Yale University, and J.D. from the Harvard Law School. The National Association of Counties has awarded him its Distinguished Service Award for his advocacy on behalf of the intergovernmental partnership.

AEI STUDIES ON FINANCIAL MARKET DEREGULATION
Charles W. Calomiris and Peter J. Wallison, series editors